WE WERE FIVE

Written by: AHMAD HASANI

Title: We were Five

Author: Ahmad Hasani

Publisher: Supreme Art, USA

ISBN: 978-1942912606

Contents

Biography

I'm Yashar. I was born in 1972 in a poor family in Lachin, Azerbaijan. My dad was working in the post office, a hard working employee he was. As a fanatic Turk man, he always tried to make a comfortable life for the family. But his salary did never meet the expenses of our eight member one. My mom was a housewife. All the time she was cooking and washing the kid's clothes, especially mine as a naughty boy the whole day. I was the second child of the family, and very interested in wooden arts during my childhood. My dad's poor work condition led me to make many of my wooden toys, sometimes for selling to my friends as well. I was good at school, one of the most hard-working students in the class. My dad liked reading, he had many books and magazines at home, sometimes he was telling us in brief, whatever he was reading, so I got interested in reading since childhood. I had so much general knowledge than my friends that I could do crosswords in many magazines as a teen.

It was at the end of my primary school days when my dad got a career and we moved to my mom's hometown, a beautiful city named NakhJawan, where I kept on my school. During the high school, I got interested in reading novels, so I read lots of works of famous writers. Jules Verne, Charles Dickens, Pushkin, Alexander Duma, and Ernest Hemingway were my favorite writers. One day I got the book "Robinson Crouse" by Daniel Defoe. It was a very amazing story, and I got such an affection of the character that I read it several times. Robinson's will was admirable and I became so immersed in the story that once I dreamed him and his island. I always asked whom these events may happen. To a high confident man to measure his will or a coward one to get experience? Maybe it happens to everybody, I was sure God's will has a philosophy with logic behind.

It was 1992. Armenia invaded to my motherland and a war was fired. My family had to move to Baku. Lots of our friends and relatives lost their lives during that ruinous war, they were living in Khojali and in that invasion they could not save their life, they had been slaughtered by Armenian forces in a savage way. They even disemboweled the pregnant women and cut the embryo's head. Those days I was a teen and insisted on fighting with the enemy together with my dad, but my family did not let me so I decided to join the army after graduation from university. My father was one of those thousand men killed during this war while defending his motherland.

Graduated from Baku University in electronic course I started my military service, two years in the navy. I was a soldier on a warship in the Caspian Sea and I learned many things during those two years that I had never known before. I did not know how to swim before the military service, but then after I was so skillful in swimming that my friends were calling me Johnny Weissmuller (one of the record winners of the world hundred meter breaststroke), an encouraging title of course. Ibrahim was the navy's commander, an admirable perfect man. Learning many things from Ibrahim I supposed myself as an experienced navy soldier.

Soon after the military service, I started my job as an electronic technician at the Baku water treatment plant, as a member in the repairing team. The plant was a very big place, treating in one hour up to twenty thousand cubic meters water of the rivers in that area. Two years later I got married to Negar, our neighbor's daughter. She was well aware of my "love of Robinson". Whenever she was out of mood of cooking, she was scrambling foods and making something to eat, called "a forest food". Her best gifts for me were models of sailing ships, my room was full of photos and paintings of islands, beaches, ships and stormy seas. All the time I wished to have the chance to experience Robinson's life and it happened to me a few years later.

It was in February 2005. I was in my office together with the other staff, drinking tea and reading newspaper. Suddenly the phone rang. It was Alireza, the head of the plant. He talked to the head of the group and asked us to meet him in his room. We were five, Morad, Habil, Ramiz, Reza and I. Ramiz was an electronic technician with a well-built body. As an experienced member of the team, he was the head of the group. Reza was a mechanical technician, a man with strong arms, all friends were calling him "A Two- Horse Power Man", and well actually he was eating for four horses. Habil was an equipment technician, a man with average height, the most talkative but active man in the group; with less salary than others and of course he was nagging all the time. The shortest and the most lovely member of the group was Morad, an electronic technician with lots of creativity in his job. Apart from different moods and personalities in the group, we were always working together all the time, we always tried to solve any problems we faced in the plant. Those days we were friendly, everything was good. I thought I was living in the best time of my life, but then after I found out how men unveil their real personality on hard days of life. Oh, and that day we were astonished when the manager called us to his room, an event never had happened before. He was a bad tempered man and we expected him to shout as usual for a weird subject; but this time there was a smile on his lips, that meant there was a different issue. He rarely used to smile. A little time passed in his room, we were confused about the matter.

-"You are wrong, this time I have called you not for an objection, but for a congratulation", He said, puffing his snip with a deep looking at us. We looked at one another.

-"Congratulation! What for sir?" asked Ramiz.

The manager started another cigarette, with a deep puff in it, he went on: "Some water treatment plants with modern technology are going to be built in several cities. Outcome capacity of the treatment in our city is going to be increased. Ministry of Power has signed the agreement for purchasing the instruments from Australia, your group is one of those selected to travel to that country for three weeks to be trained for installing, attainment and repairing the machineries. Most probably you will travel there after one month, if there is no problem, so get ready for the travel. They will announce the date".

-"In these kinds of works, technology owner country sends the equipment's and engineers for installing and running the machineries, wouldn't it be economical for the government if we had taken the training in here?", I asked.

Seems the other members were annoyed by my question, they were murmuring. Habil was beside me, kicking my leg, he said softly: "Spurning your chance?!" The manager smiled and said: "A good question. I had the same question of the general director and he said 'visiting the production line of the water treatment machines and getting training there will motivate our technicians to be more creative, also the government tries to encourage active and intellectual employees'". We were all happy and clapped.

-"Yes, you are the most competent employees of this company and I am honored of you. I had announced your creativity in this plant to upper level administrators, and they made this decision to praise you", the manager went on.

I never thought that our bad tempered executive manager, the most bad natured man on the earth, was so grateful one. The news made us very excited; it was our first journey abroad. Habil and Morad were very happy.

-"Thanks for everything, we had not known you well and we owe an excuse to you", leaving the manager's room I told him.

-"Time is a good teacher, reveals all truth to us", tapping on my back, he replied.

Still surprised by this news, we said goodbye to him and came back to our room. That night after dinner, I talked to my wife and told her the story. She was a kind woman and faced with it with ease. It was hard for me to leave her alone with my one-year old son for a few weeks, but she was satisfied with this journey for my job and feelings.

The next day there was a strange excitement among the team members, all of them were talking about their decisions. Members of the control group (operators) were jealous of the opportunity we had got; they believed that this was their right to be sent to this training tour. They even had met the manager to object, but his decisive reply that the group had been selected by the upper level administrators had disappointed them. But I knew them; all were interested in travelling and having fun instead of training and learning. One month before the travel was a good time to do our postponed works. During the time I surfed the nets to know something about the visiting places and customs of people in Australia. I was good at English, but I worked some hours to improve it, my wife was an English language teacher and she helped me a lot in this field. I did something else, unaware that it would have a remarkable effect on my future.

The month before the travel passed quickly, it was the day before the departure. We were all excited at work, our first travel to abroad have made us stressful. Habil and Morad were talking about their unfinished works; Reza and Ramiz were checking their shopping list going to buy from Australia. The manager called us to his room, giving us the tickets and the confirmation letters; he gave us the advice for the last time. We were going to join other groups coming from the other cities at the airport in Baku. The head of our group was a three member team selected by the Ministry of Power. A part of our flight was over the Indian Ocean. Habil and Morad did not know swimming, so they were a little bit anxious Always waiting for weak points of others, Reza and Ramiz were making fun of them; telling them if the plane crashed down, they would be the first passengers sunk in the ocean, their laughs had made the poor guys much more worried.

With a fake smile Habil tried to hide his fear and asked me "Yashar! Is it true the plane is going to fly over the ocean? If it crashes down, we will all be sunk".

Up to that moment, I was careless of their talking's and laughs, but his words made me laugh and I said: "What is the difference, if the plane crashes down in the sea, a mountain or a forest? Anyway, be sure to be dead, but don't think too much. We will all be safe, who says it is going to fall down?"

That day, many of other employees came to meet us for saying goodbye and wishing a good journey for us, some of the operators were seen among them, I was sure they were there for flattery and did not like to do so. We finished our job, put on our cloth and wanted to take a photo. I stood among the others and said "Don't worry; I will take care of you in this journey". Some of the co-workers asked us to buy their orders from Australia. One of the staff asked me about the souvenir and I said I would bring him a kangaroo as there was lots of it in Australia. Everybody laughed.

That night there was a strange silence in our home, just the sound of spoons and plates were heard. I had already been sent to missions far away from my family, but this journey was a different one. I thought it would take longer than expected, though my wife's smile made me feels comfortable.

-"Does leaving you alone make you unhappy?" I asked.

She sighed and said "Why unhappy! you are going to for a mission, we cannot do anything". She smiled and went on "Don't worry about us, that training will be finished soon and then we will be together again".

-"What do you want as a souvenir?" I asked. Smiling, she bends to me, kissed me and said "For you a safe journey, and then if you could, one of those gifts you always bring".

I had always given a deodorant to my wife for any events; her dressing table was full of the expensive ones. After dinner, I checked out all the packs I had made ready the day before, took a shower and went to bed. I like travelling, but that night I had a bad feeling, never wanted to see the sun shine soon.

In the morning my wife insisted on coming with me to the airport, but I did not agree with. Before leaving my wife, she gave me her gold necklace. She touched its turquoise pearl and said "the words on the stone will take care of you during the journey". I said goodbye to her and my son in front of the door and started my way. That was a hard moment. I will never forget that day, fifth of March, 2005. The milestone of my life.

Flying day

We were all at the airport except Ramiz. Habil was very excited and chewing gum, he wanted to hide his clear fear of flight. Reza had not slept well last night, it had taken him a long time to say goodbye to his wife, and he was feeling sleepy at the airport. Morad was regularly checking his watch, rumbling as Ramiz had delayed. A few minutes later, Ramiz arrived at the airport together with his wife and two sons. She had a few bags in her hands and talking continuously, it seemed she had a long shopping list. I have never seen her before; she was well built like men, exactly as like Ramiz. He always believed that she was ugly, but I did not think so, maybe he liked pretty ladies much more.

I had a small box with me on all journeys, including some stuffs like a shaver with two blades, a small mirror, string and needle, a nail clipper, and a small knife for peeling off fruits. The box was always inside a waist bag. In the luggage inspection part, I thought they would not let me take the bag into the plane, but the luggage's inspector was one of my old friends, so there was no problem. I never thought these small stuffs would give a big hand to us in future.

As scheduled, we should introduce ourselves to the head of the groups at the airport. Members of the groups together with their heads were twenty three men. Delivering the confirmation letters, one of the heads talked for a while about the regulation of the journey. Half an hour later, our plane entered at the airport. We were going to fly in a plane from Turkey to Australia with a stop in Azerbaijan on its way. It was eleven twenty when we got on the plane in which there were three hundred other passengers mainly from Turkey. I had a short glance at the passengers, men, and women, young, old. My chair was beside the window, and at the middle of the plane. Reza was beside me. Half an hour later we started the flight. The plane was good and the attendants were pretty, walking around to meet the passengers' needs. I had heard the high quality of Turkish airlines, but I had never supposed as so. We preferred to come back with the same airlines if we could. Before the flight, the pilot welcomed the passengers in different languages, also in Azeri Turkish, so exciting that some of the compatriots shouted "Long live with Turkey", "Long live with Azerbaijan". After the plane took off I closed my eyes and wished a good journey.

I opened my eyes; an hour of the flight had passed. I looked at my friends, Reza was sleeping, Habil and Morad were talking, Ramiz was reading a magazine, but his attention was with the attendants more than the magazine. One of the attendants was in front of us. I called her with a hand gesture. She came closer and said "Yes sir?" I was fluent in Turkish and I asked a glass of cold water. Smiling, she nodded and went. Ramiz was doing a crossword, he asked me some difficult items, so simple for me and I answered with ease. A few minutes later, the attendant was beside me with a glass of orange juice. She delivered the glass with respect. Her name was in her uniform, "Demet Aksoy".

-"What time will we have lunch?" I asked.

-"Half an hour", she said.

-"When will we arrive in Australia?", I asked her again.

-"Tomorrow we will be there for breakfast", she replied. She passed by.

Ramiz looked up his magazine and with a naughty look at the attendant said: "I have never seen such a pretty girl, who knows who she will get married with".

Half an hour later, they served the lunch, different dishes, and I preferred to have "chicken shawarma", a Turkish dish, very delicious it was. After lunch I was reading a magazine. Reza was a gobbler man, and he had (not) good general information. After the food he was in a good mood and asked "I heard you have read about Australia, what you know about?" I did not like his tone of voice, but let him feel free.

'Full stomach never works well, what if Reza who eats more than a man', I thought. "Yes, Australia has 7680000 square kilometer wide, 95 percent of its population is English migrants and about 1.5 percent is native. Most of them are Christian, its capital is Canberra. Sidney, Melbourne, and Adelaide are its most important cities. Its currency is Australian dollar and the country got its independence in 1901. Enough?!" I replied.

Reza was astonished and said "Well done, surely you know the language as well?"

-"So good I am at English that I can get a chewing gum from a supermarket", I replied. I was feeling sleepy and said I would sleep if he let me and then fell asleep.

I got up at four. Sometimes the plane was falling in air wells, frightening the passengers. I looked at my friends; Reza was listening to music with his cell phone, shaking the head with the music rhythm and chewing gum. The others were sleeping. I looked outside; it was cloudy and going to rain. The loudspeaker announced the temperature and outside weather condition. Again, I looked at outside. Small islands were seen in the ocean, to be honest, I was afraid of and had a bad feeling. I called the attendant.

 -"May I help you?" she asked.

-"Would you please bring a pill, I am stressful", I said.

She smiled and said "there is nothing to worry about, but I will do so". She was sedate and it helped me to feel comfortable. She came back with a glass of water and a pill.

-"Excuse me, where are we now?" taking the pill, I asked.

-"Over the Indian ocean and after a while we will be in Indonesia space", she said.

-"Are there any residents in there?" I asked.

-"Most of these islands have no resident because they have no fresh water", she replied.

-"Where can I smoke?" taking out my cigarette I asked her.

-"Do you smoke? Anyway, if you want, you can go to the restroom at the end of the corridor", she said with an astonished looking.

When she went, I put it in my pocket.

Little by little it was getting dark and cloudy. The plane was vibrating, it was clear the weather outside was bad. A little later it started to rain, sometimes together with a thunderbolt in far distances. The passengers started to worry, they were whispering. The pilot assistant's voice was heard from the loudspeaker trying to make the passengers relax, but most of them were looking outside. Reza was still listening to music and chewing gum, seems unaware of the condition. Ramiz had put aside the magazine, praying by whisper. Habil and Morad had wakened up, they looked very worried. I stood up to go to the restroom.

-"Where?" Habil asked.

-"To the restroom to be free of stress", laughing, I said.

-"Is it possible the plane fall down? I fear of that", he took my hand and with a trembling voice he asked.

I wanted to bring him in a good mood, so I whispered in his ear that "let it so, it isn't your daddy's plane!" Among all worried passengers, the face of a pretty mulatto girl with almond-shaped eyes got my attention. She looked like Cinderella, the prince of my childhood dreams. She got my stared look, so she smiled and had a greeting. Beside the restroom one of the attendants asked me to finish my job soon and come back to my seat. I washed my face to feel fresh. In front of the mirror, a lipstick and a small mirror had been left; I put them in my pocket and went out. Coming back to my seat, the plane had a harsh trembling and I lost my control and fell down on a lady who was coming towards me in the plane aisle. I got embarrassed and excused her, then I got that she was the same pretty girl from Far East drawn my attention a few minutes before. She was so beautiful that I got embarrassed. She smiled and said "That is okay" and went away.

A few minutes later, the pilot assistant started to speak and said "Please don't worry, everything is under control. Please fasten your seatbelt". Suddenly we heard a terrible sound and the plane was shaking hard, seemed a thunder passed it. All the passengers were shocked, some of them were shouting, the plane was shaking. I did not fasten the belt; I thought if there was a problem I could not open it. At that moment I was thinking just about my wife, I took the necklace in my hand and kissed it. I was thinking that regardless of all happenings, I should be safe as I had promised her to come back home. I put on the life-jacket and looked at my friends. Reza was shocked, I asked him to put on his jacket.

-"Why? Is it going to crash down?" looking at me he asked.

-"I don't know, but you should do so", I said.

He stood up and had a look around, all the passengers were frightened, and many had put on their jackets. Habil and Morad had done so earlier, so feared that they looked like dead, they had taken each other's hand. Ramiz had got his chair, praying quickly with closed eyes. I was afraid of too, but I never wanted to think of death, I was sure we would be safe no matter of the events going to happen.

Air crash

Another harsh sound and another trembling cut the thread of my thoughts. The plane inclined to the right, my heart was beating fast, everybody was screaming, I took my chair not to be thrown. I took Reza's hand and closed my eyes to feel unstressed but another harsh sound was heard and then the passengers' louder screaming. I thought a thunderbolt passed by the plane, but actually that was the second engine of the plane that was out of work though we did not know at that time. Later on we understood that the plane, taking off, had been encountered by a group of migrant birds, and their touches with the pilot's cabin and the wings of the plane had caused one of the pilot's death and had damaged both engines of the plane. At that moment we were unaware of everything, just the plane started trembling left and right with harsh moves little by little. All the passengers had lost their hope. I could not hear anything except their crying and screaming. Hard time it was, we could not do anything. The tip of the plane was downward, moving towards the ocean as fast as possible. The plane was going to crash down, but the pilot was trying to land it so safely that he would save the passengers. It was rainy and I was sure the plane would crash down. I was just thinking of God and praying him to save us, all passengers were shocked by thinking about the crash. A few minutes later, which passed as if a year, the plane touched the water intensively and moved a little extent on the water, and the skillful pilot had saved us. Seemed a part of the plane had been dislodged as a little later the water started to enter inside and filled it up to our ankles. Viewing the scene the passengers were all shocked and were crying again. Some of them were running in the aisle purposeless. I was looking for my friends. Ramiz was on his chair, unconscious with head bleeding, but Habil and

Morad had been disappeared, I stood up, looked around but I could not find them among the crowd. Reza was crying, he had fastened his seatbelt, but now he could not open it. I took out my knife and cut it. He had put on his jacket and asked about Habil and Morad.

-"I don't know, but Ramiz is unconscious and we should leave the plane as fast as possible", I said.

-"Yashar! Outside is full of sharks, they will cut us into pieces", he said with a trembling voice.

-"No difference, and inside they will cut your corpse into pieces", I said.

I hurried towards Ramiz, I released his seatbelt and helped him to leave the plane. Reza took my hand and screamed with a trembling voice he said "He is probably dead, forget him, we should save ourselves". I looked at him with irritation, although I knew that he was shocked, unaware of his speech.

-"Damn! Open the door", I shouted.

The passengers had rushed towards the all exits, some still were shocked and sitting in their seats. Everybody wanted to save himself. The attendants and the crew of the plane were helping the passengers to wear their life jackets and jump into the water. The plane was getting full of water, making it hard for the terrified passengers to pass through the aisle, like a flock out of control, they would lose their life unless they could find a way to step in. In that fanfare, an old lady drew my attention, she had her husband's unconscious head in her arms, she begged help but it was fruitless. I had torn up my tears, Ramiz was still unconscious, I left him to Reza to take him out and I went to help that old couple. I bend to take the man while a hand tapped me, "Let me help him", the lady behind me said, she was Demet Aksoy, the same attendant who had brought me the pill. She had cut her forehead, but still she was helping others.

-"You are injured, you should leave the plane", I said.

She was tired, but she said it was their duty to be with the passengers up to the last moment. I put the man on my shoulder, took the lady's hand and asked the attendant to join us and leave the plane but she said she would do so later on, while fastening the jacket of the lady. Then she went to help the others, it was a strange scene. Water had risen up to our knees and was coming up and up. The plane was moving with the waves and making our movement difficult, but we got to the exit door finally. The crowd had gathered near the exit, some were jumping into the water with no jacket. Hugging the old lady, I put the old man on my shoulder and we three jumped into the water.

It was a hard time, after all these years I can still hear the voices of the passengers, asking help, that was the worst night of my life. We were lucky to leave the plane before it was completely sunk. I turned back to look at the plane and I saw some miserable passengers who had no jacket, they were sinking in the stormy sea, those who had not left the plane were also sunk into the deep sea in front of our eyes. I had a bad feeling, I was happy as I had saved myself, but feeling bad for those who had lost their lives. I was crying while I had kept the couple together. The old woman was kissing her unconscious husband and thanked me in Turkish language, but I was crying for the other passengers, feeling sorrowful why I could not be able to save them too.

It was getting dark, the sea was still stormy. I looked at my watch, it was two hours the plane had been sunk. I was very tired and my eyes were heavy as if I had not slept for one week. We were floating over the water like a straw, moving right and left with every wave. I did not know what would happen, we were waiting for our fate. The waves had moved us far from the plane and we could not see any other saved passengers. I did not know what had happened to my friends and I was praying they would be safe wherever they were. It was a few hours after the plane crash, but the old man was still unconscious, his wife did not cry anymore, but fear of the ocean was seen in her eyes. I tried to persuade her that there was nothing to worry about and we would be rescued. The life jackets had helped us to be safe and if the storm finished by tomorrow, there would be rescue groups to save us, otherwise nobody knew what would happen.

I hugged the old woman and told her not to fear, but when it got dark I started a terrified feeling. I had no experience of swimming at night in an ocean up to that moment. It was so frightening that no one could imagine. I knew that there would be no shark or other frightening animals while it was stormy, but it was terrifying to imagine an unknown creature would swallow us. It was so dark now that I could not see the couple's face; under the thunders, I just could see the wrinkled and tired face of the old lady feeling calm now. Whenever she looked at me she said we would be rescued. The waves were hitting our faces, it was still raining. I felt tired and sleepy, but being separated by a wave stopped me to sleep, I decided to tie the jackets together with my belt to be sure we would be together even if we got asleep. For a moment I left them to take out my belt, but a wave came and passed me far from them. It was dark and stormy, I could not find them, and I just heard the old woman's crying asking me to help her. I was completely confused, I just shouted, then some other waves hit my head and I could not even hear her voice anymore. Now I was alone, nothing could do. I screamed with a loud voice calling God, then I closed my eyes and left everything to go on its way. I had no choice except to accept the fate.

I heard my wife's voice asking me to get up. I was weak, but getting warm. I opened my eyes and found myself on a beach, at first I thought it was a dream but I had really been saved. There was no storm, the sun was shining, I felt pain and my stomach was full of water, I was vomiting water. Then I stood up and looked around, I was on a tropical island, a few miles away, there was another island. My watch was out of work, I did not know how long I had been in the sea. Anyhow, I was safe. I was alone. There was nothing to do. I remembered my friends. Then I decided to walk around the beach to find the other passengers.

The coconut trees were along the beach, the sea was calm. Walking on a sandy beach was enjoyable. I felt I was in another world. I was hungry, but I took out my jacket and started walking along the beach. There was no one. I remembered my cell phone. I took it out of my pocket, hoped to make a call, but it was out of work. On my way I saw some pieces of broken wooden boats, but it did not look like a residential island. I thought if I was alone there, how it would be possible that just I had saved my life. I felt loneliness. Half a mile forward, there was a black spot. It seemed another passenger was on the beach. I walked quickly, it was true, a human being. I called him, but there was no reply. I run to him and saw that he had his life jacket, he had fallen on his face on the beach sands, I turned him back, and it was my friend, Reza. He did not breathe. I took out his jacket, started to press on his chest, but it was useless, so I had to give him artificial respiration. I repeated it several times, though his mouth smelled bad. Suddenly he moved, vomited a little water, after some coughs, he opened his eyes. I cried of happiness, he was alive and I was not alone there, he opened his eyes and looked at me and all around with confusion. When he recognized me he asked where we were and what had happened to us.

-"Tell me the truth, did we die and now we are in the heaven?", he asked.

-"Heaven! They will not let you even in hell", I said with a smile.

Then I took his arms to pull him under a tree shadow while I told the whole story. He had pain in his right leg and could not walk. It seemed he had broken his leg, so I asked him to stay there and I kept on my search on the beach.

The sea was calm and miles in far distance could be seen. It was about half an hour I was walking around the beach, but I could not find anything. I wanted to walk around the whole island. I was tired, hungry and thirsty, so I decided to find something to eat. The only thing I was familiar with in there was coconut. That was the first time I saw a coconut tree, it was high and I was not in the mood of climbing. I looked around, there were some ripped ones on the ground. I peeled them off with a knife and made a hole and drank their juice. Breaking them into pieces I ate some parts as I was very hungry. They were delicious, when I got the energy I took two of them and kept on my way.

I searched the beach up to the noon, but I could not find anything. I had reached the rocks of the beach. I preferred to take a rest under a tree, the island was green and the middle part was full of trees, but there was no sign of residence or human beings. I believed that I would have a story like Robinson Crouse except I was not alone.

Almond eyes girl

The reflection of the sunlight from the sea and the quiet waves had made a beautiful scene. It was similar to one of the pictures in my room. I always wished to be on a sandy beach the same as the pictures I had in my room and now I had got it. I thought that God loves me so much that I had achieved all my wishes, I just wanted to be with my wife at that moment. I was in my dreams that suddenly I heard a woman's cry. I stood up and listened carefully. It was from the rocks of the beach that had been extended up to the sea. I run towards it and climbed a big rock. I looked up to see what the matter was. Two men had laid down on a rock and beside them there was a woman crying. I thought they were the plane passengers so I went closer and greeted. The woman turned back and looked at me. I recognized her, the girl with the almond-shaped eyes who had drawn my attention a few minutes before the crash.

When I approached, she ran towards me, took my hand and while speaking in her own language, led me towards the two men that surely were her relatives. It was clear that they were dead and there was nothing to do. I shook my head to show my sorrow, the girl started crying again. I took the corpses under a tree and by gesture I showed her that we should bury them. She fell down on the corpses and cried again, it seemed she did not want to farewell them. She was right, maybe I would do the same if I was her. I left her to cry, when she was quiet I took her shoulders to leave the corpses and said "We should bury them".

With a piece of wood I dug a big pit under a tree far from the sea. Before burying I took everything out of their pockets and gave them to the girl. Then I pulled them into the pit and put a piece of their cloth over their face. It was a miserable scene. That was the first time I was burying a corpse, I admit it was disgusting, but there was no other way. I buried them and marked the place with stone and wood to find them out with ease later on. Then I stood and prayed for them.

It was half an hour I had finished the burying but the Asian girl was still crying beside the graves, saying some words in her own language that I could not understand. I was tired and hungry, wanted to come back to Reza, but I preferred to wait until she ended up her farewell with her dead relatives, so I sat down and waited until she became calm. I thought Reza would be hungry and could not find anything to eat with his broken leg.

The girl was silent, she stood by the graves and prayed. I cut one of the coconuts for her, she took it and drank the whole juice. She was hungry too, so she broke it into prices and started to eat. Then she thanked me in Turkish language. I was astonished how a girl from Far East could know Turkish language. I was thinking while she asked me another coconut. I nodded my head and gave her the second one. I was really confused. Finding her on that island, I was just thinking that what language I should talk to her, I was not bad in English but was not so good to speak with ease. I knew that Reza did not know any English except "yes" and "no", but now it was a different case, I was thinking when she thanked me again. I looked at her, she was calm.

-"How did you learn Turkish language? Where are you from? Who were these men?", I asked her.

-" I am Angela from Indonesia. I am 27 years old and a student of medicine, my father was from Indonesia and a philosophy professor. My mother was from Italy and herbal medicine doctor, she died two years before. Turkey had introduced a cultural program called Turkey Olympiad since 2003 to encourage youth of other countries to learn Turkish. My parents were invited to Turkey in a cultural tour for cultural programs such as poems, theater, music and so on, while visiting the country. Two years ago I had started to learn Turkish language", she said with a pleasant smile.

Then she referred to the graves and said " in this journey, my father and my brother were with me".

Again she started to cry. Angela's story made me happy and sad, happy that we have no language problem in that island and sad because of her family.

It was half an hour we were talking that I remembered Reza.

-"One of my friends is at the beach and now he is waiting for me. He has broken his leg. Can you help him?", I said.

-"Sure", she stood up, smiled and said.

On the way we talked a lot and took some coconuts. She was speaking with a strange accent, pronouncing the words in such a way that I could not help laughing. She liked reading and she knew everything.

We joined Reza, he was astonished to see Angela and said who this pretty angel was and where I found her. I introduced her.

-"The problem is that she does not know Turkish and we should speak in English, you don't have any problem, do you?" I said with humor.

-"I wished we had a dictionary here to talk to her well and enjoy her beauty", he said with a sigh.

Angela and I laughed and I said "this time you are lucky, as this angel knows our language. Say whatever you like."

Reza felt shy of his words, covered his face with hands and said, "God damn you Yashar". After some happy minutes I showed Reza's inflamed leg to Angela. She said it was probably broken and we should keep it fixed. With some wooden pieces and cloth of his shirt we made it fixed. It was afternoon, very warm and humid. We ate the coconuts, so tired I was that lying there I fell asleep soon.

I woke up hearing Reza's laughing. I did not know how long I had slept but I was still tired. Reza was talking of his diaries to Angela and they were both laughing. I looked at them and asked, "What should we do now?"

-"Before everything we should think of food as I am very hungry", Reza said.

I stood up and cleaned my pants dirt.

- "What are you going to do?, Angela asked.

-"Reza should sit down here to make a fire, you should find something for dinner, the coconut is not enough. I will go on my search to find somebody or something else", I said.

Then I gave my lighter to Reza to make a fire and started my way along the beach.

I walked for some hours at the beach, but there was no sign of the crashed plane and its passengers. It was strange as if our plane had crashed somewhere around, the waves should bring some pieces of the plane or of the passenger's stuff. Perhaps the crash had happened far from there, so it was a miracle that we were alive. It was afternoon and it would be completely dark after two hours. I did not feel good and the sunset and loneliness had made me depressed. There was something near the beach moving with the waves, I walked towards, took it, a red baby' shoes, it reminded me the plane, I was unhappy, surely it belonged to one of the passengers. I sat down by the sea, and remembering the crash scenes I cried. I remembered my wife and son, surely they had heard the crash news and they had thought that I was my dead. I was crying while I felt a hand over my shoulder. Angela had been worried about me. She sat down beside me, I showed her the shoe, and she became sad and said something in her language.

-"Why are you depressed?", she asked.

-"You are lucky! There is nobody to worry about you", I said.

She frowned and said "Am I lucky? You have somebody to live for".

Her words were interesting and full of energy. I felt better. 'We will be rescued, we must be rescued', I thought. I felt energetic, not depressed anymore. I remembered my wife's words, always saying "you can". We came back near Reza. The fire was seen from a distance. He had made a stick for himself. Seeing us from far distance he came forward a few steps and asked about the other passengers. Angela shook her head that we were alone on the island.

Angela had made dinner ready, a few tropical fruits and some seashells, all new for me. The fruits tasted strange and the shells had been cooked on fire, something like soft-boiled eggs with a strange taste, never experienced before. They were disgusting, but little by little I started to enjoy. After dinner, we sat around the fire and were talking about the island, animals attack, other passengers, and rescue groups that maybe would come to find us. We decided to leave Reza there to keep the fire burning, I and Angela should keep on our search and go around the island to know it better. I asked Angela about the wild animals on the island, I knew that there were tigers and lions in Sumatra, one of the biggest islands of Indonesia.

She said she did not think that there would be any wild animals there because most of those islands were volcanic, even some were as new as one hundred years old. But we should be careful and before searching the island, we should have something to defend ourselves.

-"Snakes? Crocodiles? Are there any?", I asked.

-"I don't think there is a crocodile here, but surely there are snakes", she replied and went on, "in the forest we should be careful of poisonous snakes, they hang over the trees and then jump on the other animals or human beings and sting them, or the pitons, they move around the hunt and break its bones and then swallow it alive".

Reza was fearful of snakes, he had sweated and had stared at Angela. She had noticed his fear, it was enjoyable for her. When I was doing military service as a navy I had seen how a big snake stuck on a piece of wood on water and floating over water arrived at a land in a far distance. Even if the island was volcanic, maybe some snakes had come to the island by the storm.

-"Don't you think we should all stay here and wait for the rescue?", Reza said .

-"We will stay some days at the beach up to rescue group's arrival, but we have a few problems", I said with a smile.

-"What is the problem?", he asked.

-"Drinking water and a shelter", I replied.

-"In tropical regions, it rains a lot, there would be no problems of water for drinking, but we should have a shelter. Perhaps we would be safe of wild animals but we would feel uncomfortable under the rain which lasts for some days", Angela said.

-"What should we do if nobody comes to save us, can we save ourselves or they will bury us with no corpse?", Reza asked.

I put my hand on his shoulder and said that I did not know how and when we would be saved but we would. This was our fate that we were still alive and I was sure that we would come back to our family. "Family", Angela sighed and said, looking at the sea. I got sad, I had forgotten that she had lost his father and brother, we had buried them that morning. I wanted to excuse her, but Reza asked me to forget about it. The sea was calm and a mild wind was blowing. The moon was reflected over the sea and had made a romantic scene. I wished I was there with my wife, who knew how she had faced with my death news. I took out my cigarette, they were still wet. I put them beside one another on a rock near the fire to be dried. Angela was looking at me and the cigarette with surprise.

-"Better than nothing! ", I said.

Although wet cigarettes taste awful, but as I was alive and could breathe, I felt that I was smoking the best cigarette of the world.

I got up early in the morning, the sun was shining. I went to the sea to wash my face. I stood by the sea, it was beautiful and a cold breeze made me feel fresh. I was thinking of the events happened. Was it a disaster or an opportunity? So far I had read lots of books about psychology, one of them believed that all happenings, even a miserable one have a philosophy, full of heaven's favor. Although at that moment I had seen no sign of that philosophy, I felt that I had a gift from heaven as I was alive and had two friends there. I thought that God loves us so much that he had sent us to that island to enjoy the nature and holiday.

Perhaps he wanted us to be alone like Robinson Crouse and make a close relationship with him. Of course we should wait for the future to know what the facts would be and make the heavens clear for us. I thought we should wait for the rescue groups as much as possible; and if nobody comes to save us, we would find out a solution. I could not accept that island as our homeland forever.

I came back to my friends, Reza was still sleeping, but Angela was not there. At first I was worried, but later on I guessed where she could be. I was right, she was beside her father and brother's graves, praying in her mother tongue. I went closer and started praying. When she finished her praying she looked at me. I said good morning and smiled as a reply.

-"I was worried the cannibals had taken you for breakfast", I humored.

-"Don't worry, there is no cannibal here", she said. " Has Reza wakened up?", she asked.

-" He was sleeping while I was coming, but right now he has already woken up. We should come back soon. Snake stories we told last night has made him worried about us, he thinks a boa has already swallowed us, he will have a heart attack", I said.

We laughed and started walking. On our way, she was talking about the tropical fruits, like Papaya, Rambo tan and Lychee that I had never heard even before. Also, she named some birds that one could hunt, but they were living in the island forest that we could not go there due to our unknown condition. We were busy talking when we found ourselves near Reza. He was still sleeping. I woke him up. He yawned and said "what do we have for the breakfast? The seashells we had last night were delicious, could you find out more?".

I threw one of the coconuts on him and said "Get up! We are not here for a holiday. The fire is off, make it on soon and put some wet grass to make smoke maybe somebody sees us, we will go for searching at the beach". I said these and started my way. A little later Angela attached me while she had two coconuts in her hand and asked "How can Reza make a hole in the coconuts while he has no knife". I looked at her seriously and said "let him have a hard time to think that we are not here for a holiday".

Angela's secret

We were inspecting everything at the beach carefully. Everything was useful at that condition. Beside the sea, we saw some pieces of broken boats or old wharves. I was throwing them to the land, I thought they could be useful later on, while we used them to write "S.O.S" and "V", the international signs for asking help, so big that could be seen from the sky. I was sure if a plane passed by the area, they could be seen. We walked for two hours, it was an enjoyable talking too as Angela had good general knowledge and was talking Turkish with an interesting accent. On our way we had to pass the rocks, she had no shoes and should be careful, she had taken my hand not to slip. There was a white sticky material on one of the rocks which drew my attention. It was interesting. Angela explained that this was a kind of sea algae that when it was dry it would get very hard so the locals used it as a real stick. On a part of the beach there were hard rocks we had to pass, they were very slippery and Angela could never pass them, so I had to hug and pass her, I felt shy but it was clear that she had no problem with this feeling. We passed by the rocks and went on our walking on the sandy beach.

There was a mountain in the middle of the island, its peak was the highest point of the island and if we could go there we would be able to have a look around the island and far more distances of the ocean. I was thinking this when Angela pressed my hand and showed me something in front of us by the sea. We run towards it. When we arrived, we saw one of the passengers, it was clear that he had died a long time ago. We pulled him under a tree to bury. We took all the stuffs he had. His watch was still working, it was ten. I wore it and put my own out of work watch in my pocket. It was a wedding gift from my wife, it was priceless for me. He had a knife in his pocket too, I wondered how he had taken this into the plane. I put the knife in my pocket and gave my little one that was just for peeling off the fruit to Angela. She was so happy that like kids was jumping. She kissed the knife several times and put it in her pocket. Then she sat down in front of me, took my hands and kissed them, saying something that I could not understand. I was completely confused and did not understand the meaning of her works. She was bending in front of me as if she was worshiping an idol.

-"Stop it Angela! A little knife has no price to thank so much like this", I said.

-"Yashar, you do not know what you did", she said with a smile.

I asked the reason of her works, but she did not reply and I did not insist on. I thought maybe this was their custom to thank this way for a gift, maybe if I had given her a better one she would have danced for me. I decided to test it one day.

I looked at the identity card of that passenger. His name was "Kamal Ozgour", 29 years old and from Turkey. He was good-looking and I was sad to see he had lost his life at that young age. I decided to keep his stuffs and if one day I found his family I would give them back. I took off his new shoes and gave to Angela. It was clear that she was unhappy to wear a dead man's shoes, but when I said I could not hug and carry her anymore, she had to put them on. His burying was a difficult work for me, I cried for him a lot as he had died far distance of his family and hometown.

We were praying for Kamal that suddenly we heard a sound like a plane. It was sunny but there was nothing in the sky. Angela was happy and said "surely the rescue team has seen the smoke of the fire, let's go back", we took up our stuff and run towards Reza. Rescue happiness was seen in Angela's eyes. I was happy too and thinking that when we got in the first telephone center I would call my wife. We were very tired, but thinking of being saved had given us energy, and we came back all the way in twenty minutes that we had walked in several hours. Unfortunately, when we attached Reza we got disappointed, he was sleeping, and there was no fire burning. Viewing the scene I lost my energy and fell down on the sand and punched the sands angrily. Angela was so irritated that could not help her and kicked Reza.

Reza cried painfully and shouted "damn! I am sleeping".

Angela shouted "you stupid, now it is not time of sleeping, didn't you hear the plane? We had asked you to make smoke so that they can find out us".

She started crying and set aside. Seeing his mistake, Reza got ashamed. We were all silent for half an hour. Reza had made a fire and tried to put green grass on it to make smoke but it was useless, the plane had already gone and there was no sound, except that of the waves and seagulls. I was out of a mood, I remembered the knife, took it out and looked at it. It was amazing, so strong to kill a wolf with. I stood up and after looking around I found a tall tree with smooth branches. I cut some of the branches and started to sharpen them while Angela attached me. I looked at her, she was better than before.

-"You were right about him. He is lazy", separating the cut branches she said.

-"These things happen, don't think about, if you want to save your life, you should rely on yourself, do whatever you think is right." cutting the woods, I said.

-"I don't know why, but I trust you and I am sure you will save us from this island", touching my face, she said.

-"Thanks for your trust. Be sure, we will be saved from here", looking at her, I said

She smiled with satisfaction and changed the topic quickly and asked "what are you going to make with this wood?".

-"To catch a fish", I said.

An hour later I was ready to jump into the water with ten wooden lances to catch fish. That part of the beach we had lodged was sandy and it was impossible to catch a fish, so I had to look for a proper place. I asked Angela to stay with Reza, but she did not accept, she insisted on coming with me and I accepted. Reza was still feeling ashamed of his mistake and had stood by the fire and looking at us. We started the way.

-"How could we go out the island if nobody found us?" Angela asked me.

-"By an ocean-travelling ship", I replied.

-"Making fun of me?" she said.

-"No, I am serious, if we have some tools we can make something like that", I replied.

-"Where can we get the tools. What a pity my cell phone does not work otherwise I would call to bring saw, hammer and nails?", she said and laughed.

-"If we have to make tools, we will do it, you know the needs are the mother of inventions", I said.

She looked at me and said "well done"!.

We arrived at the rocky part of the beach that we had passed in the morning. Big and small rocks had been expanded up to the water. Standing on the rocks, I could dominate over the fishes. I stood on a rock and waited for the first fish. Angela was looking for crabs and seashells. There were lots of small fish and I could catch them if I had a fish net or even a butterfly net. After a while there were a few big fishes. I threw the lances towards them, but no success. I tried it times and times, it seemed ridiculous. I tried it for one hour, but I was unsuccessful and I had lost the lances too. I was tired and hopeless, suddenly I got an idea. I cut the lances in four branch shape by the knife, the first throw got the point. I shouted happily and showed the fish to Angela. Lances cutting was an interesting innovation and I could hunt even the small fishes. In half an hour I had caught some fish and joined Angela. She had found a big crab.

-"Have you ever eaten these crabs? They are really delicious, tonight you are my guest for dinner", she said.

We were very tired, so we sat down on a rock to take a rest. I wanted to smoke, but it was clear that she did not like smoking.

-"Don't you know that smoking is bad for your health?" she asked.

-"Why not, I know, I promise I never smoke in this island when the box is finished". We both laughed.

Mysterious cave

It was six in the afternoon and we were still sitting on the rock. It was getting cloudy and we were going to have a rainy night.

-"It is clear that we can drink enough water tonight", I said.

-"How? With a glass? Maybe you mean we can stand under the rain and open our mouth! Or maybe we lie on the ground and...", she said this and started laughing.

I was very upset, I could not believe that she had been friendly with me to make fun of me. I had a sense of humor, but I did not like making others fun.

-"If you think deeply, you will see that it has a solution as well", I said while giving an angry sidelong look at her. I said it and turned my face.

-"I am sorry", still laughing, she said.

-"My father believed that human beings are respectful with any idea and thoughts and we should always respect them. He did not like making others fun", interrupting her words I said.

Angela excused me a lot and said that she did not want to bother me, but I was still upset. A little later the rain started, so harsh that I had never seen before. We jumped down the rocks to find a shelter. We were running along the rocks while we found a hole in the middle of the rocks, it was the entrance of a cave. Big rocks had fallen beside each other and had made a cave. We made a torch and entered in. It was not too big, but three to four men could stay there. At the end of the cave there was a hole upwards, making the cave light. It was a strange and unnatural place, I could not believe that it had been made by natural factors. Maybe it seemed meaningless, but I believed that God had made it for us. We were looking around the cave with curiosity. On one of the rocks there were some words in an oriental language. I showed them to Angela but she could not understand anything. On the floor of the cave there was coconut peel, I gave one of them to Angela.

-"Yeah, someone has eaten coconut here", confirming me she said.

-"I know this, I mean the cutting edge is smooth, it shows that someone has cut it with a knife or a sharp thing", I said.

On the floor, there were old bones of a hunted animal, it was clear that somebody was living there. We found three empty bottles and some cans too. The cans were old, but there was a date on one of them, surely it was the date of the manufacturing. I cleaned it with my hand, it was "1943". I showed it to Angela, she said with surprise "oh my God, it means they date back to the Second World War?!". She showed me an old rusty cartridge. I was sure there was a military force, but it was unknown how many they were and why they were there.

It was six in the afternoon, and it was still raining. I stood at the cave entrance and put my hand under the rain to drink water. Angela brought one of the coconuts peel and washed it with rain.

-"You said we should think well"; filling it to drink, she said.

She filled it with rain water and gave it to me. Then she filled all the coconut peels and the three bottles. During the two days we were there, we tasted the fresh water for the first time. I looked at the bottle, it was interesting as in daily life there were many bottles around us, but we did not care them, while they are valuable and we should keep them safe.

-"We should think of fresh water if we are going to stay there", I told Angela.

-"What should we do?" she asked.

-"To find out many more bottles or making a wooden barrel or something like this", I said.

-" So we should look for every corner of the island", she said.

The weather was awful and we had to stay the night there. We had good food and a warm place, but I had a bad feeling. Reza was alone and it disturbed me, but then I thought I should punish him for his mistake, so I preferred to leave him alone until the morning. I decided to move him to our new place. It was good and we could make it a suitable place for living with a little change. But it was not a safe place for a long time because I knew that there were lots of tsunamis there and beach life could not be safe. After dinner, I sat beside the fire and started smoking. We had passed two days there and still I could not believe all the happenings. All were like a dream for me.

-"Hey, what are you thinking about?" Angela asked tapping on my back.

-"I wished all these were just dreams", I replied.

-"Even if everything is a dream, I am a fact.". Then she asked "what are you thinking honestly?", she smiled and drying her hair by the fire, she said.

-"All these happenings are very strange for me. I think this island like the mysterious one in Jules Verne stories and I think we may face with strange things", I said.

-"What do you mean?", still drying her hair, she asked.

-"God has not sent us to this island without any reason, he has a purpose for that, I am sure we will stay here up to when all truth would be clear to us", I replied.

She was amazed and a little bit annoyed of my speech so she said "what do you mean by staying here?".

-"I mean that nobody will come to rescue us. That is my feeling" I replied.

She was much more amazed and asked " Do you mean we will live here for the whole of our life? What kind of philosophy may it have that we live here without any news of anybody and then die here?".

-" I wish somebody came and saved us, but I feel that we will live here for a while up to know some truth and then we will find out the way to go out of the island", I said.

-"Although my father was a philosophy professor, I am not interested in that field. Just tell me you will save us from this island or not?", she asked.

-"Of course we will save our lives, be sure even if I have to swim across the sharks I will save you", I replied with a smile.

She smiled and kept on drying her hair. I remembered the lipstick and the mirror, I had found in the plane washroom. I took them out of my pocket and gave her. She was very happy and cheered, then she said something in her language that I could not understand, just I knew that she was thanking. It was clear that she was not as happy as when she got the knife because she did not show the same behavior. While drying her hair, she was singing a song in her mother tongue, I was very tired and it was like a lullaby, soon I fell asleep.

When I woke up it was six in the morning. I thought the watch that I had taken from the dead corpse yesterday had been set with Turkey time zone so I set it at eight. I got up and went outside, I found Angela standing on a rock and trying to catch a fish. When she saw me, she waved hands. It was sunny and the sea was beautiful. I went by the sea and Angela came beside me. She had caught a fish. "I am not bad at catching fish", with a raised eyebrow she said.

We had breakfast. Angela stood up and said "what should we do right now?".

-" I will go on my search, you should go and bring Reza here. Make a fire near the cave, make smoke too, maybe somebody finds us", I replied.

Although I knew it was useless and nobody would come to save us, I felt my words had made her annoyed last night, so I decided to make her hopeful. She insisted on coming with me, I touched her hair and said "Reza needs our help, especially as he is hungry now and has spent the whole night under the rain. If I will not come back at night, don't worry, I try to finish the island searching until tomorrow evening, I hope to find something. I promise to take you next time".

Angela accepted my suggestion but it was clear that she wanted to be with me. I took two of the bottles, she took my hand and with a meaningful looking said "takes care of you. I am waiting for you". I said goodbye and started my way.

I was walking beside the sea and looking at everything carefully. The wooden lance and the knife were the only things to defend myself, so after a while I decided to make an arrow and an arc to hunt a bird for lunch. When I was a child, I was making lots of them, but this time it was different. I had to make something to hunt with. After a while I could find out a tree with smooth branches. I used my shoelaces as the arc chord. Making an arc with ten arrows lasted one hour. When they were finished, I tried them out, I was dissatisfied. The arrows were not thrown well as they had no feather at their end. I was looking at the trees, there were beautiful, strange birds I had never seen before. I was throwing the arrows to any bird I could see even to the colorful parrots, but it was fruitless, just made them escaped. I decided to be brave and enter the jungle.

It was noon, the weather was hot and humid, the insects were bothering too but I had to bear. In one part of the jungle there was a land full of birds like partridge. I hid behind a tree and threw all the arrows, but none of them hit the point. I had no more arrows, I was hopeless. Suddenly I got an idea. I had already read Australian Indians used boomerang for hunting animals. It was a curved shape wood, they used to throw it towards the animals, it was spinning in the air, hitting the point, and coming back to the hunter. Of course I had never seen a real boomerang and I could not make one, just I could use the throwing technique. There was a wood on the ground looked proper for my decision. I took it and threw towards the birds so that it spun in the air and moved parallel to the earth. The wood moved roaring in the air, it attached the birds, they were frightened and escaped, but the wood had hit two of them, they were paddling on the ground. I stood up quickly and run towards them, they had been injured. I took off the knife and cut the heads. I was so excited that I took the hunted birds in the air and screamed joyfully like Indians. That was my first hunting on that island, I was very happy. I went back to the beach to wash them. Now I had food and feather for making arrows. I was so hungry that I wanted to eat both of them together. First, I roasted the wings, they were delicious. I wanted to eat more, then I remembered Angela and

Reza, so I decided to keep some of the meat for them. I hang over the rest of them from my waist and started my way along the beach.

It was three in the afternoon when I arrived at the rocky beach. The rocks were too high to pass over so I had to pass through the forest to reach the peak in the middle of the island. From the peak I could see all over the island. I had no experience of walking in a tropical forest by myself, it was really difficult for me. I was ready to defend myself with arrows. I was thinking of the snakes hanging over trees or wild animals that may come to me. I admit that it was scaring. Seeing me, some of the birds were screaming with fear and flying over that made me frightened too, some of the trees had some long wooden strings hanging over, I took one of them and pulled, they were rough. Some of the trees had fruits like melon. Everything was new and interesting for me there, from the colorful parrots to the strange fruits of the trees. Some of the trees had beautiful fruits, but I did not dare to test, especially as Angela had advised me to be careful. I wished I had brought her too, as she knew many things about the tropical regions. I arrived at the densest part of the forest, passing across the dense trees and bushes was really difficult but I reached the hills. The forest was not so dense, as it was before, so that I could see around the island. It was evening and I was very tired. I wished I had a cup of hot tea, especially those my wife was always making. I sat by a small tree and started smoking. I remembered my wife and son. My poor family, surely they were mourning for my death. I must not lose my hope, I had to attach them even if this story wanted to last some years. I knew that God helps his creatures and in that condition just God could be helpful. I begged God to help me and this made me feel comfortable.

After a short resting, I stood up and continued my way. After two hours the sun was setting down and I had to reach the peak before the sunset. I arrived at the peak when it was eight, half of the sun was behind the ocean and the red sky confirmed that it would be a quiet night, one with lots of stars. Form the peak I had dominance over the island and I could see miles of the ocean. I could even understand the shape of the island and the four geographical directions. The island was like the left foot palm with four toes stuck together. The distance between the big toe with four others was like a small bay as if a small hunting ship could pass through without being seen. Before it was getting dark, I made a big fire and I was sure it could be seen from far distances. I roasted a piece of the meat for dinner. It was blowing swiftly and the moon picture over the sea had made an amazing scene. I wished I could share the joy with my darlings. I was so tired that fell asleep soon.

A sign from the inside of the forest

I got up with the sun beams and seagulls sound. As usual, I checked the time, it was eight. I could inspect the island better as it was getting lighter. I estimated that the cave we had found out yesterday was in the southwest of the island, and facing with the high rocks I had come into the forest from the northeast of the island. The bay head was towards the north. I thought if we could make a sailing boat and move in the north and the northeast directions, we could reach the cargo ships passing route in a very short time and we could be saved especially as the wind was blowing from the southwest to the northeast. I was looking around to find a proper place for our living, to have more control over the island and to use its facilities. Suddenly there was a light shining from the east of the island, among the tree branches. It was the sun beam, but I could not see how it was shining and who was making it. I hid quickly behind a rock, I thought there was somebody else on the island. There were lots of questions in my mind and my heart was beating fast, perhaps it was one of the passengers or the island Indians, or a pirate or one of those stayed on the island since the Second World War. It was possible because I had heard once there was a Japanese soldier, "Hiro Onada", who was unaware of the end of the Second World War after twenty nine years. He had been left alone in one of the islands of Philippine, who was taking care of the ammunitions by himself and he was shooting to the island residents. It was undesirable to think of fighting with a man or group of men as I had just the arc and arrows and the knife with myself, and so far I had never killed a man, I did not know what to do, finally I decided to go there secretly to see what the matter was.

I came down the mountain quietly. I had to crawl and sometimes to crouch to pass the bushes to enter the jungle. Keeping the knife in my hand, I was standing behind the trees and controlling all around well. I was very stressful. Half an hour later I arrived the place where I had seen the light, but there was no light and no human being there. I had nothing to cut the high bushes in front of me, except a wooden stick to pull them aside, the insect bites were awful. The trees of that region were very tall, some of them were even taller than fifteen meters. I spend a little time looking for the origin of the light, but there was nothing, except the birds sound I could not hear anything. I was very thirsty. I sat down by a tree and wanted to drink one of the bottles, when I looked up I saw something among the trees and bushes. I went closer and passed the grasses aside, I saw an airplane, the bushes around showed that it had been crashed down a long time ago. The plane had been covered by the tropical plant and only the screen was seen, I thought the light reflection was due to it. I passed aside all the plants with my stick, the plane was now clear, it was a rather big war plane, the red circle on the wings showed that it belonged to Japanese forces during the Second World War. There were lots of holes in its body, I thought that it had been crashed down because of the allied forces fire. I opened the door with difficulty, in the cabin there were two corpses of the pilots. They had been corroded and just their skeletons were seen in their uniforms. At the end of the plane there were lots of metal and wooden boxes, they were a little bit safe after fifty years. I was curious about their contents. I opened the boxes, it was amazing. They were full of Japanese rifles together with cartridges and spears, hand grenades, mortars and their guns and in brief ammunitions of an arsenal. There were some broken empty boxes too. I thought if somebody else had come here and used these. Anyway, it was unbelievable for me as the other things were untouched and safe. I got one of the rifles and pulled its trigger, it moved with ease. I was happy to find these out, I kissed the refile and looked up to thank God for his kindness, and then I wanted to test it. I put some cartridges inside and went out of the plane. I shot an air bullet, the sound was so roaring that the birds flew the air due to fear. It was so loud that I was sure Reza and Angela had heard it as well and surely they had been worried. Although I did not want to leave that plane, I preferred to take another rifle with some cartridges and come back to my friends. I wanted to tell them the story of the plane. While I was leaving the plane, I stood and looked at it, I did not want to leave it, and I felt that it was just a dream.

Coming back, I was feeling powerful and brave. I was so happy that I could face even a dinosaur. I had a rifle in hand and another one on my shoulder, my pockets were full of cartridges. I was sure that my friends would be surprised and never believe the story. With those ammunitions we could defend ourselves. Finding out the plane and the ammunitions, I was hopeful and I knew that if we looked for more we could find out much more interesting things. Perhaps it was a mission from God to find out lots of secrets on that island.

I was so excited of my discovering that I did not know when I had left the forest and come back to the beach. From a far distance, I could see the smoke of the fire my friend had made. It was noon and I was hungry. I wished Angela had made something for lunch. Arriving the cave I called Angela, she came out quickly, seeing me she waved hands and run towards me. She came closer and hugged me and asked "Yashar, are you okay? I heard a shot and I was worried about you".

-"There is no problem, I came back as I had promised, safe and sound", I said.

She hugged me again. Touching the rifles on my shoulder, she went back and looked at me and the rifles with surprise.

-"Where did you find out them, man?", she asked.

-"Inside the forest, it is a long story, I will tell you later, first of all give me something to eat I am very hungry", I said.

She took my hand and like a mother taking her kid, she took me into the cave. On the way I asked about Reza and his broken leg.

-"What a friend you have, he eats like an elephant and he orders, he thinks I am his servant. He disturbed me a lot in your absence".

Hearing this I got annoyed. Before entering the cave I thought I should put the rifles out of Reza's sight, I asked Angela to wait out of the cave. Entering the cave I saw Reza roasting fishes on the fire.

Seeing me he said "hey man, are you fine?", with no excitement in his tone. Eating one of the roasted fishes, he kept on "oh, where were you up to now, I was worried, I heard a shot and thought you had got a problem, I wanted to come for help but you know as my leg is broken.... You know how I feel now, and I could not send Angela by herself.", he said and went on eating.

I was annoyed of his carelessness. Around him there were lots of fruit peels and fish skeletons, it was clear that he had not a bad time, he had eaten like a horse.

-"Yeah! It is clear you were worried, do you need anything else?" I asked.

-"I am so thirsty if there would be two fresh coconuts....", he said.

-"It is clear Angela has made you lazy. Do you think here is a three star hotel?", I said.

-"As she is here it is a five star hotel not a three star one, she is cute!", he said laughing.

I was so irritated that I did not say anything and left the cave. I sat down under a tree. Angela came with two grilled fish in her hand and sat down beside me.

-"Don't disturb yourself, he understands like this. Eat these and then tell me what happened up to now in the forest and what you found out", she said.

Angela was a stranger, but she was so kind to me that I felt comfortable with her.

-"Before anything, take these birds and roast them, they are very delicious. I hunted them yesterday. Believe me, I hunted them just by throwing a wooden piece", I said.

I was happy to see that she was interested in listening to me. While she was making fire for roasting I was eating the fishes and telling her all the story of the plane and what had happened yesterday. After lunch, Angela told me how she had taken Reza into the cave and had served him like a servant.

-"I wished you had not helped Reza and he had died there", she said.

This made me unhappy and I said "a good human being should be good all the time, and the other side's bad behavior should not change his personality" I said.

She looked down and excused me for her unreasonable talking. She then said "so what should we do right now?".

-" If we want to save ourselves, we should look for the island very well and collect all useful things and then make a plan", I said.

-"What useful things can we find out? "She asked.

-"I don't know, but I am sure if we search well we will find something. The first was the Japanese airplane. Do you know that with all these ammunitions inside the plane, we can defend ourselves against the pirates?", I replied.

Hearing this Angela was pale and she swallowed the spittle. I noticed that her hands were trembling, but she did not want to admit it.

-"I am right, even the pirates cannot....", I said. She stopped me talking and while her voice was trembling, she said "don't talk about them. They are wild and dangerous, nobody can stand against them", she said.

-"How do you know? Ever faced?", I asked.

-"Once when I was ten I went to my uncle's house in a village to take care of their little son for a while. They were farmers and due to work on the farm they could not stay at home. Their village was near the sea. One night the pirates attacked the village and killed many in front of our eyes, including my uncle, as he wanted to stand against them. They took many women and children as well...." She said while crying.

I put my hand on her mouth to stop her talking about this bad memory.

-"While I am alive nobody can hurt you in this island. Be sure!", I told her while I was cleaning her eyes.

She smiled and hugged me, although I did not want to but at that moment I could not do anything except touching her hair. A few minutes later she was calm, she cleaned her eyes and said "sorry, I did not want to disturb you, but I could not help myself. I have no good memory of them and I never want to face with them again". I knew that she had not forgotten the story and all her words were due to her fear, so I smiled and said "the pirates will never find us. We will leave this island as soon as possible".

Angela tricks

It was four and a half in the afternoon, we had laid down under a tree by the beach. Feeling lonely Reza came out of the cave and limped towards us while he was very angry. I was bored of his laziness and irresponsibility and I wanted to talk to him, so when he sat beside me, I said "Reza, I liked you so I saved you, I still like you and you are dear to me. Here we all have the same condition, so nobody is superior to others, nobody can abuse the others". Getting the point of talking, Angela left us and went away to be busy with the trees and bushes.

- "Since we have come here, you have done nothing, and you have forced Angela to do your works. Don't you think these are sorrowful behavior. I expected you more than this. If you want to leave this island you must do your best, but if you want to live here and enjoy yourself, you should know that we have to leave you", I said.

He did not expect these words from me, so he got irritated and said "I have broken my leg and I cannot do anything, you know this that I cannot...". Meanwhile Angela shouted loudly and jumped out of the trees. She was running towards us and screaming "escape, a tiger, a tiger...". I was completely confused as I could not believe that there would be a tiger in that island, but I stood up immediately. When she attached us, she took my hand and said "escape, the tiger is coming". We were running towards the cave. Meanwhile, I saw Reza, he had taken aside his stick and running with us to come into the cave. Angela stopped running and pulled my hand to stop. I got the point that she had lied. Reza entered the cave, a few minutes later, he came out quietly while he had a hunting spear in his hands, and we were laughing at him. He said "come inside soon, why you are standing there?".

Angela and I were still laughing. He shouted "why are you laughing? Are you making fun of me?".

-"You are running well with a broken leg, you have deceived us these few last days", laughing, Angela said.

Reza saw that we knew everything. He was confused and said " my leg is still painful, I had to...". But we both were still laughing.

In the evening, I took a fishing spear to catch a fish for dinner. Angela came with me.

-"What should we do tomorrow?", she asked.

-"I will go to the crashed plane to find some more things, you should stay here as you know the plants of this region well, you can find useful things for us", I said.

She looked innocent and while she had rolled her lips, she said "if I stay with Reza, I have to do his works. And I cannot go into the jungle by myself. But if I come with you, I will not fear and I will not be worried of you".

I knew she was bored of Reza so I accepted her suggestion. Talking about food, Angela asked "how did you hunt the birds by a piece of wood?". Telling her the whole of the story, I said "do you like to take a rifle and hunt some birds for dinner?". She accepted with joy and we came back. I did not want to talk to Reza, but I did not want to make him worried so I went into the cave and told him that we wanted to go hunting. I asked him to catch fish if he could. Reza did not say anything and turned his face, I knew that he was still annoyed. I put fishing spear by the cave and we started our way into the jungle.

On the way Angela continuously was talking about Reza's fear and running, she was laughing. I laughed as well, but then I thought my friend was being scorned and I should get a better way to justify her issue. I was sure Reza was doubtful about us and it happened in a short time.

A few minutes later we entered the jungle, in one part of the jungle there were lots of bamboo, some of them were taller than ten meters, we would use of them. I had already read in a magazine that how hunters in Peru had made a big ship with bamboo and straw and had gone fishing in "Titika Lake". If we had the tools we could make a forest house, a wharf, and a boat. Angela had good knowledge about bamboo, she even said the sprouts would help blood cholesterol setting, food digestion and controlling blood pressure. Along the way she was talking about medical features of bamboo sprouts with eager. But all I was thinking was how to cut them.

Although passing through the jungle in hot and humid weather was very difficult, I did not feel it as I was talking to Angela. She had a good knowledge and was talking about each of the trees; food and medical advantages. I was astonished by her knowledge and asked about the reason. She said her mother's ancestor was all doing medical practice. She was showing me the edible and non-edible and poisonous seeds and she was explaining about them. She was very brave and did not fear of catching forest frogs, too disgusting for me to watch even. She showed me the poisonous and non-poisonous ones and explained how hunters used to smear their poison on the tip of their arrows for hunting other animals. We had gone hunting, but it was practically a scientific tour, we were so busy talking that we had forgotten why we had gone there. Then we found out that it was evening and we had to come back with nothing. On the way it was blowing and it was clear that we would have to pass a stormy night.

When we arrived at the cave we saw Reza standing with his stick by the cave looking at far distance. It was clear he was out of mood of eating and sleeping and being alone. When we went closer he grinned and said "I see you have had a good hunting". Then he brought his head closer and made fun and said "it is not too bad far from the family! A non-residential island, a pretty girl with almond-shaped eyes, how romantic it was, seems you have gone hunting, have not you?". I was annoyed by his way of thinking about us and said "why are you unhappy? You had enjoyed more than us. You were free and you could at least catch fish for dinner". Feeling he was right, he said "no, I was not free, I was here to signal if a ship would pass". Angela stopped him talking and said "maybe with this stick, isn't it? Don't make tired yourself. In a stormy weather nobody comes here to save you. Come inside the cave, it is going to start raining". Then she said something in her language that her face showed it was a darn.

We entered the cave. The fire had almost been finished, so I put some woods and made a big fire. A few minutes later it started to rain and Reza came and sat down by the fire while he was depressed. We filled all the coconut peels and the bottles with rain, we drank as much as we could as we knew there would be no fresh water for a few days. We ate some jungle fruits for dinner, one of the sweetest fruits I tasted for the first time was "papaya", something like melon and bigger than a hand palm. Yesterday I had seen lots of them in the forest, but I had not touched them even, as I feared they would be poisonous. After dinner Angela was busy cleaning the cave. Outside it was a little bit cold and sitting by the fire was enjoyable. I lighted up a cigarette and laid down by the fire. I was thinking why Reza wanted to be lazy and did not do anything. When we were in the company, he was lazy, but here we had a different condition and I expected him to be with us to solve the problems. Reza knew that nobody wanted to speak with him so he went asleep. His look was saying that he was doubtful of us, thinking that his doubt may make him do something wrong was disturbing me. I was busy thinking that I felt a warm hand on my shoulder, it was Angela, sitting beside me and looking at me with her pretty eyes as usual. Since I had given her my knife she had been so friendly with me, I did not want Reza to understand us so I asked her in English "what is the matter? Don't you think that your behavior has been strange." Smiling, she shook her head and said "no", but I was sure she had been changed and was too much kind. I knew that people of the Far East are very kind but not so much like this, she was familiar with the language and culture of Turkish people, she should know that in our culture a strange man and woman should not be so close to one another, especially as I was married. Anyhow, I should be careful otherwise there would be a fight between me and my friend. I thought I must hint her to control her behavior. I thought that it would be okay if I talk to her tomorrow and explain everything so I asked her swiftly "do you want me to show you the plane tomorrow?". She was still looking at me with her magic eyes and while she was smiling, she nodded her head and moved eyelashes to show that she agreed. She was really pretty especially that night as she had combed her hair. I was really confused by her strange behavior, I preferred to sleep soon before she wanted to be more kind. I turned back and slept by the fire, but I was thinking why she had changed her behavior.

Tomorrow morning Angela woke me up and we came out of the cave quietly. We wanted to move before Reza got up, so we took two bottles and the rifles and started our way to the jungle. On the way Angela was talking about everything and I was just listening. It was nearly ten and I was hungry and tired. I wanted her to take a rest and eat something.

-"What is the matter? Why don't you speak, is there any problem?" after a short breakfast she asked.

-"You should tell what the matter is", I replied.

Seemed confused, she asked "I don't know what you mean".

-"It is just a few days we have got familiar with one another, you behave as if we have fallen in love", I said.

She laughed and said "Who knows? Maybe it would be true".

I was astonished and asked "What do you mean?"

-"Nothing, just kidding", she said.

-"Angela, there is no doubt you are kind and friendly, but you are so much kinder and this makes others to be curious, I don't want anybody to be doubtful of me and...", I went on.

-"Do you mean Reza? If you think of him, I want him to be doubtful forever, I don't live for others so I never mind them", stopping me talking, she said.

Talking to her was useless and I had to avoid her in practice, so I stood up and we kept on our way.

Night inside the plane

Half an hour later we arrived at the crashed plane. Angela had been astonished by seeing the plane and when she saw all those ammunitions she said something in her language.

-"Hey man! With all these ammunitions we can have a good life here", taking one of the rifles, she said.

-"But I think another way, I think with all these we can leave the island as soon as possible", I said.

It was clear that she was unhappy of my words so she changed the topic and said 'thanks them as they have left all these for us".

-"Not all of them, just two of them, of course their corpse" and then I went to the pilots' cabin. Angela followed me and when she entered the cabin and saw the reminded skeletons she had a disgusting feeling, then she frowned and said with irritation "God knows how many of my people had been killed by these cruel forces". All Indonesian islands had been occupied by the Japanese forces during the Second World War, and through the stations they had made in these islands they had been doing military actions against the warships and submarines of the allied forces.

-"If you agree we should make them tidy and count them, we stay the night here and tomorrow morning we dig a pit to hide all these ammunitions", I said.

-"Why should we hide them?" She asked with surprise.

-"At least we can be sure that Reza cannot touch them to do something wrong, we will take them out and use whenever we need, before anything we should bury the corpses to make their soul feel comfortable, then they will let us sleep in their plane".

-"They were our enemy, their corpses should be thrown in front of dogs", she said with an angry tone.

-"Every corpse should be buried with respect, no matter who he was. You are tired, I will do it myself", I said.

By the spear I had taken from the plane I started to dig a pit a few meters a side. It was a difficult job in that part of the jungle than the soft sandy beach, I was sweating. Angela had sat down by a tree and looking at me, as she was out of mood, she came and stood by the dug pit and said "you have buried so many corpses in these last days".

-"So what?", I asked.

-"I mean you have got so much experience that after coming back to your homeland you can continue this work, I am sure you will be a famous funeral man" and she laughed again.

I did not like her sarcasm and to make her irritated I said with a serious tone "you are right, I can get a good salary, but before coming back to my homeland I wish I had the honor of burying your corpse" and started laughing. She did not expect to hear such a reply so she smashed a bunch of soil over me and went away. I laughed so much that made her angry, and while she was saying some things in her own words and I was sure that they were darn, she turned back to the plane.

After one hour, digging the pit was over. The corpses belonged to forty or fifty years ago, to avoid their decomposition, I wrapped them in a piece of cloth that was their parachutes and put them beside each other into the pit. Before burying I took their identity cards and whatever they had in their pockets to deliver them to their families. In one of their pockets I found out a family picture showing the pilot by his parents. A young man about thirty, smiling and hugging his parents with honor, but right now he was nothing except a bunch of skeletons. Since coming to the island I had buried some corpses and I had been sad for them, but this one hurt me so much that with every bunch of soil I was putting on them I was crying too. I knew Japanese are Shinto followers, but I put a cross on the graves to find them with ease later on. I prayed for their souls as well.

It was four in the afternoon. I was very tired. The weather was very hot and humid. Although Angela was giving me fresh fruits, I was still hungry. I had not had any mood for anything except to prepare something to eat. Therefore, I started searching in the same area. Due to the guns I had, I came back with some hunted birds half an hour later. Angela had cleaned inside the cabin and had made a fire in front of the plane. Seeing me she came some steps forward and put a piece of papaya in my mouth and said "take a rest, I will make something for eating". Then she started to grill the birds on the fire. She was very active and behaved in such a way that I felt she was enjoying to give service to me. We took a rest after the lunch and then just collected wood for the fire in the evening. After dinner Angela said "cleaning up the inside of the plane I found out something, I think it would be interesting for you". She went into the plane and came back with a Samurai sword. I took it, the scabbard had been a little bit rusty, but the blade was so smooth that I could see myself in it. It was very sharp after all these fifty years left unused there, sharp enough to cut a cow in half. We could cut bamboos with and make whatever we wanted.

That night we slept in the plane. Angela had put together all the ammunition boxes and the parachutes on them to make something like a bed. It was not as soft as a bed but better than sleeping on the ground.

But I preferred to sleep by the plane exit to be far from her. Angela had noticed my mind, said with a sarcastic tone of voice "do you sleep on the floor at home?". I looked at her and said "no! I sleep on the bed and of course with my wife".

She pretended it that did no matter for her and went to sleep. I was sure she had noticed what I did mean. From the jungle we could hear the sound of night- hunting animals. Angela had been afraid of, so she asked "do you think the corpses soul disturb us?".

-"Take it easy, we have a samurai sword and a full gun, nothing can hurt us", I said.

Before sleeping, I took the sword out of its scabbard once again, its blade shining in the fire flame gave me a strange feeling of comfort. I knew the sword was a gift from the soul of the soldiers I had buried respectfully that day, I kept it and slept comfortably.

Tomorrow morning Angela had already wakened up and was busy making breakfast with tropical fruits. Seeing I had got up and watching her, she came with coquetry like flight attendants and said "dear Australia passenger, good morning, the breakfast is ready to be served". Then she put the fruits in front of me with a smile and sat beside me.

- "Did you sleep well at night?", I asked.

-"It was not bad but I wished you were…", she said with coquetry.

I looked her seriously, she changed the topic quickly and continued " we can live here with a little change. What do you think?"

- "Not bad, but it has no view over the island and we are unaware of the happenings around us, if we take the stuff out of the plane, we can have a temporary place for living. I think we should have a place for life on top of a hill ", I replied.

-"Why a temporary place? "She asked.

- "We don't know the island and we don't know what will happen in future, so if we have several places for living we will be safer.", I replied.

We decided to take many things out of the plane after the breakfast and bury them. Digging a pit for thirty four boxes lasted up to noon. We put them in the pit, covered them with a parachute left on the plane to keep them safe of the humidity and then covered all with soil. Then we covered the plane with branches of trees. Now there was nothing to worry about.

A sign of the opposite island

Coming back to the cave we cut some bamboos with the sword. I wanted to make a boat with to go around the island, especially to those unknown parts. Carrying the gun and the sword I was feeling myself as one of the Japanese soldiers in the Second World War, except I had no fear of the enemy's attack. I was going forward and sometimes I was shooting in order to hunt a bird. Suddenly Angela took my hand and pointed to a bush shaking in a near distance, it was clear from the movement of the bushes something had been hidden behind. We thought it as a wild animal going to attack us, so we pointed the guns to shoot towards. Angela shot first, but it hit a tree in the bushes. She wanted to shoot the second time, but it was my turn. I had pointed the gun to the middle of the bushes and then exactly when I wanted to pull the trigger, a man came out of the bushes. His hands were up and while he was shouting "Don't shoot! Don't shoot!" in English he ran some steps towards us, then he fell down as he was too weak to stand up. We ran to him. He was an old man with some torn clothes. Clearly he was one of the passengers on our flight wandering these last days on the island. Angela checked him up and said he had not eaten anything these days. I carried him on my back and we went to our cave.

We arrived at the cave around noon. Reza had leaned in one corner taking a nap. The fire had been finished and the cave floor was full of fruits peel and fish skeletons. I put the old man on the ground, he was still unconscious. Angela asked me to make a fire and bring some coconuts. I left the cave quickly and came back with the orders a little bit later. Reza had wakened up and was looking at Angela and the old man with astonishment.

-"Who is he, Yashar?", he asked.

- " We found him in the jungle, maybe he is one of the passengers of the plane", I replied.

Angela was pouring coconut juice in the old man's mouth. Drinking the juice he got the energy and opened his eyes a little bit. He looked at us and with a weak voice said in English "food, food". Angela asked Reza if there was anything for eating, he looked around with confusion and said "I don't know, I have not eaten lunch yet". Then he stood up and started searching among the fruit peels accumulated on the cave floor. As a physician Angela was thinking herself responsible for the old man's health, so she shouted angrily "God damn you! Go and catch some fish, he is hungry".

-"But my leg...", Reza said mumbling.

Angela looked at him with irritation and Reza understood he should leave the cave. Then she looked at me and said "Darling, can you make something for eating?". I smiled and picked up the gun and left the cave. Half an hour later I came back with two hunted birds and some fruits. Reza had caught some fish and crabs too. I did not expect him. When we came back the old man had already got his conscious and could speak, although he was very weak.

- "Do you know where he is from?" Reza asked Angela.

-"Yes! He is American, one of the passengers like us...", Nodding the head, she replied.

-"American! Do we have to speak with him in English?", Reza interrupted her and asked.

-" He is a retired professor, he was travelling and busy of his scientific studies, and now he is here with us", Angela paused and said.

While they were talking, I made everything ready to grill the fish and the birds, we gave some fruits to the old man as well to feel fresh. It was lunch time, the old man was eating so greedy that clearly he had been hungry for these last days. I did not feel very hungry, so I preferred to give my food to him, he was doubtful to get it but finally he did. Angela put some of her food in front of him, then we both looked at Reza. He did not like to do so, but with our gesture and against his will he accepted to share some of his food. The way the old man was thanking showed his politeness.

After lunch we asked him to introduce himself more. He looked at us deeply and said "thanks indeed! You saved me. My name is Jim. And as the lady said I am a retired professor in geology from the John Hopkins University, Baltimore (a city in Maryland State in America). My wife "Shargeh" is from Iran and my daughter is Sarah. Due to my job, I travel to many countries and do geology researches. I was going to travel to Australia and now I am on this island with you".

-"What have you eaten in these days?" Angela asked.

-"I could just break two coconuts to eat, it was really difficult. Yesterday I had to eat a strange fruit, but it made me feel bad. I was resting myself behind the bushes and if I had put on my pants a little bit later I would have lost my life", then he started laughing.

We were laughing too. It was interesting that Reza was not understanding anything but was laughing more than us. Then Angela started to introduce us, Jim was listening to her carefully, he was a little bit fat and bald but good-looking, he was very polite too. While he was talking to Angela, he took his wife and daughter's photo out of his pocket and showed us. His wife was similar to Chinese rather than Iranians, but it was clear they were a friendly and lucky family. He had his family's photo and while kissing it he was crying. That scene reminded me my own family and I went out of the cave. Reza that had not got anything of their talking so he followed me. I laid down by the sea, Reza sat beside me and was drawing with a stick in the sand. It was clear he was not so happy of meeting Jim.

-"Where did you find out the guns?" he asked.

- " In the forest beside the corpses of two men, it seemed they had died a long time ago", I said.

- "Interesting! Can I have one?", he said.

- "What are you going to do with?", I asked.

-"Well, both can go hunting", he thought and said.

As I knew he was afraid of snakes I closed up my eyes in half and said "can you go to a jungle full of dangerous and poisonous snakes?". He had believed me and said "ok, forget about it".

- " Was there anything especial yesterday?" I asked.

He took some stones and while throwing into the sea carelessly said "no. Not any especial happenings just I saw a light reflection from the opposite island, but it happened just one or two times, I don't think it would be important".

Hearing this I hurried into the cave, took my binoculars and one of the guns. I looked at the opposite island with the binoculars, but there was nothing, I shot two times and then looked at again. I saw one jumped out of the bushes while he was waving his hands to get our attention. Angela and Jim came out of the cave with excitement. She asked the matter and I said "there is one on the opposite island. Give me your mirror to signal him with light". I took the mirror and while I was looking at the opposite island with the binoculars I was reflecting the light too. He had got our signal and was waving with more excitement. The distance was too much to recognize him clearly, but I guessed he was one of the passengers. I was sure it was the best day of his life. Jim had a bad experience of being alone on the island. He put his hand on my shoulder and asked me to help that man in any way I could.

Our distance was about six miles, although I was skillful in speed swimming, without considering the sea animals attack, it was difficult to swim all the way. And we did not know how many people were there on that island, probably some of them were injured, if so they could not swim. The best thing was to make a boat with wood and bamboo and to go there, but it was evening and after a while it was getting dark, so we postponed the work to tomorrow morning. After eating dinner we talked more about going to that island. We decided that tomorrow Reza and I would go to the forest to bring wood and bamboo. Angela and Jim were going to make rope with tress leaves and barks. It was clear Jim was very happy of this suggestion, but Reza was dissatisfied. Tomorrow morning I wakened up Reza with difficulty. Jim was still sleeping, but Angela had got up early, gone for making breakfast. I took one of the guns with the sword, Reza wanted to start the work after breakfast, but when he got my insistence he accepted to join me and we started our way into the jungle.

Arriving in the bamboo forest, Reza was surprised with all those trees.

- " Wow! We can do many things with all these bamboos", he said.

- "Yeah! But if you don't limp and if you are not lazy", I said.

 "What are you saying? I had broken my leg. Do you think I was limping decisively?" he said with a surprise.

- "I don't think, I am sure", I said.

- " Can you prove it?' he said with a grin.

-" A broken leg normally takes two months to be recovered with a proper nutrition. And the day Angela said we should escape of the tiger, you were running faster than us. Look man! You should not think yourself smart and the others stupid. We are all in a bad condition and we should work together to find a way to save ourselves from this island. And one more thing, I am loyal of my wife and will be. There is no relationship between me and Angela, I don't like that you would be doubtful of me. Okay, that is enough, we should eat something and start our job".

When Reza got that I knew everything he said nothing and sat quietly beside me. It was the first time I was working with a samurai sword, it was very sharp, and working with that was not tiresome but very enjoyable. After cutting about sixty of the bamboos, I started to cut them again into pieces about four or five meters. This time Reza asked me the sword to test. He took it in his hand, looked at it carefully and said "long time ago I watched a movie named "Seven Samurais" (the director was Akira Kurosawa), all the time I wished I had a real sword". Then he started cutting the bamboos. He was making so strange movements and voices like samurais that led me to laugh a lot. Then we divided them into fifteen piece packages and tied them with the rope we had made by the tree branches to carry them to the beach on our backs.

The packs were a little bit heavy. Since living on the island, it had been the first time Reza was under pressure, he was nagging all the way. He was tall and well-built and in our plant we had done much more difficult jobs before, but I did not know why he wanted to be lazy here and he was thinking these works were a kind of labor works. Maybe he had hit his head on a rock in the plane crash and he had lost his mind. Anyway, we carried the packages all in four times to the beach. It was tiring. When we finished the job, Angela helped us feel fresh with two grilled fish. They had made lots of ropes by twisting tree barks. Angela was very skillful in this work and had taught Jim too. She was a real sample of eastern girl and I was sure whom she would get married to, would be lucky. After lunch Angela came with a smile and sat beside me. Without any words she showed me the ropes. I tested them. They were rough. I told her well done and she left me without any words, but her meaningful looking made me thinking. Eating enough food Reza seemed restful, he belched and said "making a rope does not have any honor! Does it?". I was not in a mood to reply to him, but I was sure we would see all her skills through the time.

We tied all the bamboos together with the ropes and made a raft of two to four meters with two paddles. It was finished in the afternoon, but we could not start the way as after a few hours it was getting dark, so we decided to make a little food and go to the opposite island tomorrow morning. Finishing the raft we all had stood beside and expressing our ideas.

- "How are you going to carry the fruits and food up to the island?" Reza asked.

He was right, carrying even a few coconuts in a raft was a difficult job. I had not thought about it.

-"I remember once a noble man told me when one thinks he has no physical problem" Angela told me and fetched the basket she had made with leaves and barks.

She tied it to one of the paddles. Her intelligence had made all of us surprised. We all thanked her. She had made the basket skillfully. We talked about our plan in details at night. Reza was always thinking for himself, he said "I hope they would not be so many as making food would be difficult and there is no space for more people in the cave".

- "If you catch fish, there will be enough food for you" Angela said with a frown.

I had decided to go to the island by myself, but Angela said there would be sick or injured among them, so she should come with me. Her idea was good and Jim confirmed it too.

New guests

When I got up in the morning Jim and Reza were sleeping. Angela had already left the cave. Coming out of the cave I saw that she had put some fruits in the basket and was catching fish.

-"We don't want to travel for a few days, we want to come back up to the evening", approaching her I told.

Throwing the caught fish on the land she said, "Who knows? Maybe it would be stormy and we would have to stay there the night".

She was right. We put all the stuffs in the basket and started the way. I took the gun too.

The weather was great and after passing a few days on land, paddling was enjoyable. We had stood on the raft as the water had covered it. I thought I should consider this point making a boat to leave the island. Due to the paddle the raft was moving very fast.

- "Did you make breakfast for Reza?" I asked Angela.

- "I am not stupid anymore, never want to serve everybody, bad or good", she said while laughing.

-"So which one am I? Bad or good?", I asked.

- " You are something else", she said with a smile.

Then she looked at me without anything, just nodded her head. I knew what feeling she had about me, but I had to pretend I did not; otherwise her love would be troublesome.

A few minutes later she laughed loudly and said "oh! Think just in which language Reza and Jim will speak together, maybe as the deaf", she laughed again.

We had passed half of the way when Angela pointed to a point in the sea with horror. The back fins of some sharks were out of the water as they were following us. I was shocked. That was the first time I saw a real shark. They were big and frightening. God knows how many passengers they had eaten so far. I gave the paddle to Angela to move swiftly and I took the gun to shoot. We had a gun, but we had to be more careful as I had heard an injured shark could be more dangerous.

-" What should we do if they attack?", Angela asked with a trembling voice.

-"Don't worry! I am ready to shoot, if they attack just hit them with the paddle on their beak as their weak point", I said.

We passed them quietly. They maybe had not seen something like our raft, or perhaps they were not as hungry as they swam around us for a while and then passed by. An hour passed.

- " Do you think we can make a boat with these bamboos and leave the island?", Angela asked.

-"Leaving the island involves making something stronger and bigger to resist against the sea storms that is impossible for us now, and we have to take food for some months", I said.

- " Some months!", she said with a surprise.

- "We don't know how many days we will be on the travel, we should be careful and take much more food. You know Reza, if we have less food, he will pass away before everybody", I said.

- "I think we should not hurry up, if we solve fresh water problem, here is not too bad. We can enjoy life up to rescue's arrival" I said with a humorous tone.

Angela did not care and to show she was relaxed, she shrugged her shoulders.

-"I don't have anybody. I just say for the sake of you to come back to your family otherwise I can live here with you forever", she said.

She was trying to show her love with her every word and action, I wondered how she had been in my love in a few days. I was thinking when her voice cut the thread of my thought. She showed me the island in front of us where an unknown man was waving his hands waiting for our arrival. I paddled quickly. We had to raft a few hundred meters more when he jumped in the sea and attached to us by swimming. We took him out of the sea. At first I did not recognize him, but looking carefully I got he was my friend, Ramiz. He was very weak, but alive and I was thankful. I hugged him and kissed his forehead happily. Angela was looking at us with a surprise as she did not know him. I introduced Ramiz to her and asked him about Habil and Morad.

-"I don't know, I can't remember anything about the crash. I was unconscious when it happened and I don't know how I came out of the plane. When I got conscious I saw myself with a young man from Turkey. His name is "Hakan", he said with a weak voice.

I asked him about Hakan. He said the man had fallen down under a tree unconsciously due to starvation and he could not move. Ramiz also was weak and could not speak well. Angela gave him a little food and I started paddling. When we arrived at the beach Ramiz pointed to a part of the island, I saw he was showing where his friend had fallen down. I asked Angela to be with him and I run quickly towards the young man.

I found Hakan among the bushes, falling down on his face on the ground. I took him up. He was a young good looking man around thirty with wavy hair, but perhaps a lazy one as he had been hungry for these few days without doing anything. They had not made fire or caught fish even. I carried him on my back and coming back to the raft I was thinking how more intelligent the prehistory human beings were than these two men.

When I attached to the raft, Ramiz was good. I asked Angela to take care Hakan.

-"Have you gone around the island well?", I asked Ramiz.

When he shook his head, I knew I was right about my friend. He was very selfish and was never thinking about others, he had presented his personality while we were working in the company. I thought there would be other people on the island too, so I asked Angela, "What do you think about going around the island?". She showed her agreement with a smile as usual.

Adding two other men to the raft made paddling a little bit difficult, but as Ramiz was helping me I was not too much tired.

- "Where were you in the plane crash, Yashar?", Ramiz asked.

- "In the plane!", I said with a smile.

He smiled too and said "no, I mean, what were you doing?".

- "Why do you ask?", I said.

- " I remember when I had a little conscious I could hear two men talking beside me. One said we should save him, but the other one said 'leave him. He has already passed away'", he replied.

- "Do you remember them? Who were they?", I asked.

- " No! But I feel they were familiar", he said.

I knew the whole of the story, but as I did not want to make a stress between him and Reza, I just said "don't think about these things more. Everything finished. Be happy, we are all together". I changed the topic and said " uh! Reza said he had seen the light reflection from the island you were. How did you do this?"

- "I got a dead fish at the beach. I did not think it would be useful", he replied while laughing.

We paddled around the island for an hour but could not find any interesting things. It was clear that there were not any men there. I checked the whole of the island with my binoculars to see if there were any corpses. In our religion burying dead ones has oblation, meanwhile the stuff in their pockets help to know them better and inform their family with ease later on. When we arrived on the other part of the island I shot several times, but there was nobody else there.

-"Oh man! Where did you find these?", seeing the gun and the binoculars, Ramiz was surprised and asked.

-"A long story. I will tell you.", I replied.

I had worked with both Reza and Ramiz for several years, I knew their character that they were not reliable and whenever it was necessary they had preferred themselves to others. I remembered how Reza wanted to leave his friend in the plane crash. Surely if they knew the presence of all those guns and ammunitions, they would use them against us one day. I had asked Angela not to say anything to anybody about them. Finding nothing on the island we started our way to our own island to arrive in before the sunset and join our friends. Coming back to the cave, I was all the time looking behind to see if there was anybody to save. Due to all the food and drink Angela was giving to our guest, Hakan got his strength and could speak. He was a good looking man, a leather merchant who was doing business with Australia and on his way to this country he was now on that island after the crash. He was a good man, I had been tired of paddling so he got the paddles to go on. I sat down beside Angela and started eating and taking a rest. It was clear that she was not happy. I asked the reason, but she said it was just because of rafting, but I felt she wanted to be close to me.

It was sunset and we had not too much way to pass. The wind was blowing and we should arrive at the beach before the storm. Seeing Reza and Jim, who had made a fire by the sea, Ramiz stood up and started waving. He was too excited that told Hakan "Let's help paddling to reach soon". We were all paddling. Arriving the island, Ramiz and Hakan greeted with Reza and Jim. Angela and I pulled the raft under the trees at the beach to be kept safe from the storm. Reza was very shocked to see Ramiz but tried to pretend his happiness. I felt he was completely ashamed. Joining them Jim tapped on my shoulder and showed his satisfaction with a smile.

That night we had a heavy rain. We were all around the fire eating the food Reza and Jim had prepared. Eating enough warm food, Reza and Ramiz started talking, laughing and telling their memories to Hakan. He could not understand many of them; but joining them, he was laughing too. Everybody was busy, I looked at Angela, standing by the cave entrance, she was filling the coconut peels and the bottles with rain water for our drinking with no care to others. Then she took one of the bottles and without paying any attention to others, she sat down in front of me. Her hair was wet but she was still attractive. While she was speaking in her mother tongue and nobody could understand it, she drank a little of the bottle water and gave it to me to do so. The others were shocked and just looking at us, but it was understandable for me as she had already done such a strange movement in front of me when I gave her the knife. Anyhow, I took the bottle and drank a little. To stop any misunderstanding of the others I said "as I have saved her, she thanks me all the time. You know the people from far east". The way Ramiz and Reza were looking and whispering showed that they had not only believed me but also were very doubtful.

Although that day I had saved the two men and I should be happy I was impatient as I felt hearing one calling me from far distance and asking me to help. Angela had sat down by the fire beside me and was drying her hair.

- "I feel you are not okay and something bothers you", she said.

"Maybe you don't believe, but I hear somebody asking my help", I replied.

- "Perhaps you remembered the plane crash seeing Ramiz and Hakan", she said.

- " I don't know, but all the time I hear a woman's crying. She asks me to give her a hand", I said.

Reza tried to show me by the gesture to look at Ramiz sitting beside him. Ramiz was famous of ogle in our group, he had stared at Angela with his mouth open. Suddenly Reza tapped his back and said "you had too much for dinner, wasn't that enough?". And we all laughed. Ramiz was ashamed and after a little mumbling, he said " no I mean she has got wet, it is raining heavily, and I should have a look outside" and we laughed again. Jim said goodbye and went to sleep in a corner. Then I asked Angela "Giving water to me, what were you telling? What are all these strange movements for?"

She had a naughty look at me and replied "I was thanking you for all things".

- "Don't you think they were doubtful about us?", I asked.

She smiled and with a special coquetry said "let them do so! Then what?". She stood up and went to talk to Hakan in Turkish. I didn't believe Angela as if she wanted to thank me she could do so in Turkish. Anyway, I took a cigarette out of my pocket and started smoking.

Reza approached me and whispered, "He had already died. How did you save him?".

Puffing up the cigarette I looked at him and said "if you had made your favor, he would be with us from the first day".

He got my sarcasm so he said he was so tired of catching fish that preferred to sleep. He went to sleep beside Jim. I felt tired, so I put aside the cigarette and went to sleep there.

Last survivor

When I got up in the morning the others were still sleeping. Angela had laid down beside me putting her hand on my chest. I put her hand down quietly and left the cave. The sun had already raised and the sea had a unique beauty. The fresh air of the beach and the sound of the seagulls were enjoyable. I wanted to wash my hands, I heard again the help voice and again I started the uncomfortable feeling. I should do something. I looked around. The raft was still there, safe from the storm of the last night. I decided to go around the island. At first I decided to go with Angela then I thought I should be alone. I went into the cave, took some food and my gun and the binoculars; and put the raft on the water. A few miles away, I watched the cave with the binoculars. Jim and Angela were beside the sea and Angela was waving me. I knew that she wanted to come with me and was unhappy to be left there, but it was good for both of us.

After one hour of paddling to the north I got the bay mouth and led the raft to the right hand to move inside. The trees had been extended up to the beach. The colorful birds were singing in such a way that I felt myself in the heaven. The sea was so clean and blue that I could see the bottom pebbles. I was astonished why such a beautiful island had no residents. I wished my wife and son were with me. I decided to take them there one day to believe me as I could not describe its beauty. It was getting warm and the water motivated me to swim a little, the hobby I had never done since the day we had arrived in the island. I was alone, but I enjoyed the swimming for two hours. It was noon when I left the bay and kept on my way. The only thing I was thinking was Ramiz and Reza and the improper acts they maybe do in my absence. I knew that Ramiz's presence could make Reza much more incompatible. I was afraid of standing against them one day.

It was two in the afternoon when I arrived at the most northern point of the island, similar to the big toe, a place with huge rocks approached up to the sea. The sea was hitting strongly to the rocks and I had to observe my distance carefully as the raft was not a reliable one, it could be broken down hitting the rocks. Paddling the raft I saw a yellow color piece floating on the water, I watched with the binoculars. It was a piece of life jacket. I shouted "is anybody there?". The sound of water hitting the rocks was louder than my voice. I shot and then checked among the rocks. Suddenly I saw a hand, raised up weakly and waving me. I jumped into the water and swam towards the rocks. It was difficult to swim among the rocks by the beach, especially when it was stormy but as I had got training during the military service as a navy I overcame the problems with ease. I went over the rock, I found a woman, weak with no energy to move, her lips were dry and her face was thin. I sat beside her, I pulled away the hair off her face and recognized her. She was "Demet Aksoy", the flight attendant who tried to help the passengers up to the last moment. Her left leg was bruised, looked broken. I took her into the water to swim quietly to the raft. As I had forgotten to tie the raft somewhere at the beach it had gone away a little but we got it at last with all difficulties. I took her on the raft and gave her some fresh fruits. We moved towards the cave. I could not go on the search as her health was more important. We should leave there as soon as possible to ask Angela to visit her leg.

Half an hour later demet was in a good condition and started speaking.

- "Thank you for the help", she said in Turkish, then she introduced herself and asked "Do you live on that island?".

I laughed and said in Turkish "no! I was one of the passengers and you spoke in English with me for the second time".

She looked at me carefully and said "let me know, aren't you the man wanted to save the old couple? Could you do anything?".

I shook my head to show sorrow. She asked again "Are there any other people on this island?"

I was confused, so I replied shortly "yes!". Demet was one of the most beautiful flight attendants and although she was weak, still looked pretty. I thought Ramiz would lose his control seeing her and do improper things. Only two things could stop his bad behavior, being far from him; and his bad tempered wife.

At the sunset we arrived in the west part of the island. Seeing the other people and the fire they had made at the beach, Demet was very glad. I showed the cave and said "They have come to welcome us. They will be happy to see you". When we arrived at the beach Hakan and Ramiz came into the water to take the raft out of the sea. Ramiz' looking made it clear that he had come just because of curiosity not to help. All of them came close to see the new passenger of the island carefully, to see how she had been alive after all these days. But Angela had stood in a corner with a frown. I asked her to visit Demet. She took Demet's hands without any talking and took her into the cave. She was angry with me.

Seeing Demet's beauty, Ramiz touched my hair "Man you are great! Where did you get this mermaid?".

I was so hungry and tried that I was not in a mood of replying, so I just asked "is there anything for dinner?".

- "Be sure we will never have any problem of food and drink while this girl with almond shaped eyes is here", Ramiz said with a laugh.

Then he started describing Angela's beauty and some racy words. I did not listen to his worthless talking, picking up the stuff from the raft I went into the cave.

Now another man was added to our population, so we preferred to eat the food out of the cave by the sea. They had caught many fish and collected many seashells. Colorful local fruits had made the dinner to look perfect. Demet had sat down beside Hakan with her leg in a splint and was talking about the plane crash, how the plane had been on the route of the flying birds, leading it to crash down. Hakan's looking showed he was very happy to see his compatriot in that group. Reza and Ramiz were just looking at her beauty and clearly did not understand too much of her words. Angela had sat down beside Demet and was listening to her while helping her in eating, whenever I was looking at her, she was turning her face away to show her wrath with me. Finishing the dinner, Demet thanked for the food and said "maybe you don't believe, but tonight I ate the most delicious food of my life, in all these nine days I was among the rocks I was just crying and asking God to help me. I had believed that I would die, but at the last moment I heard a voice saying 'we have sent you a help. Raise your hand'. I owe my life to you", she said while crying.

I couldn't believe that the voices I was hearing all the last night were all inspirations. I had been shocked. I had a strange feeling and everybody was looking at me.

That night Jim did not join us for dinner. He had sat down by the sea. I thought he was upset about something so I took a grilled fish and approached him.

-"The sea is beautiful, you prefer to enjoy yourself!", I said giving him the fish.

- "No! Being alone is better than being with some people that you cannot stand their behavior", he said with a smile.

- "What happened?", I asked.

- "The boys made Angela fun of in your absence", he said.

I got red.

-"Angela was unhappy as you had left her alone. I warned them several times, but they did not listen to me. To be honest, I am afraid of ", he went on.

-"Fear? Fear of what?" I asked him.

-"Fear of fighting with each other instead of thinking about saving ourselves. Sorry, but your friends are not good ones".

Even Jim had noticed the wicked personality of my colleagues but as I did not want to talk more about the issue I said "No. Please don't think that way, they are friendly, but okay tomorrow I will talk to them and warn them to feel more responsibilities", I replied.

-"And what will happen if they don't accept?", he asked.

- "Be sure! Nobody can do irresponsible things while I am here on this island. Everybody should know his duty", I replied.

-"You had promised to take care of me all the time, so why did you leave me alone with these evils?" a little later Angela joined us and said

- "I did not want anybody to doubt about us. If we want to be together all the time it may….", I said.

She interrupted me and said "Let it happen! Let them think whatever they want. I know you well and I am sure of myself. I never want to be with them anymore. Yashar, you promised me to take me from this island, if you leave me alone with these...", she started crying.

Jim hugged her to console. She was right, I should not leave her alone.

Big decision

When I got up in the morning, there was no fire. The others were still sleeping in a corner. I took the fishing lance and got on the raft. A few miles away there were lots of fish. In a few minutes I caught a few and came back to the beach. Angela had wakened up and together with Jim they were busy of making fire. Seeing me she approached, her smile meant she had forgotten what had happened yesterday. She took the fish and we went to grill them. The grilled fish smell made the others to wake up and come by the fire. Reza and Ramiz had slept late, they did not want to wake up soon, they were mumbling. A little later Angela helped Demet to join us. Seeing them Ramiz turned his face to Reza and Hakan and said "Oh! If you had told me I would have brought her hugging, isn't it boys?", and they all started laughing. Demet was unhappy of his words but did not care him and joined us by the fire. Reza took a grilled fish and putting it on the fire to be cooked well said "hey boys, have you ever thought how many mammal birds there are in the world?".

-"One is the bat, I don't know the others", Hakan said.

- "The other one is a flight attendant!", Ramiz said and they all laughed so that Demet got annoyed and went to the cave. Jim had not understood their words, but he noticed that they had made Demet fun of, so he warned them in English to control their behavior.

-"Thank you Angela, this is a perfect breakfast", Ramiz said while taking another grill, then he told Reza and Hakan "hey boys, would you like to go swimming after the breakfast, here is one of the best places of the world for holiday and enjoyment".

Eating a grilled fish Reza said "Angela, please take some seashells and crabs for our lunch, if there are some fresh fruits, it will be wonderful", and they laughed again. Angela got red and wanted to say something that I stopped her to let me talk. I started my talking with comfort and said "my friends, don't behave in a rude way, although it is a far distant island here with no resident, we are all educated civilized people so we should respect each other. Angela has helped us so far and we should thank her, now we are many and we should accept that making food for seven persons is a difficult job and one cannot do it by herself.....".

-"Now there is a pretty flight attendant among us, her duty in the flight was serving the passengers and now here they could work together to give service to us, why are you disturbed?", Reza interrupted me.

-"First, they have no responsibility here. They could be kind, but they are not our servants; second, we have many works to do here and we should share them otherwise we have to stay here for a long time", I said.

- "We are free here and nobody can order us, we spend these few days in a way we want. I am sure they would come to save us in a few days. Who are you to order us?", Ramiz said with a serious tone.

-"Since you have come here to this island you have done whatever you wanted. I can't stand your irresponsible and rude behavior and leave here. Who wants to enjoy himself the whole day can stay with you!", I said.

-"Damn! If all of you leave here I will do whatever I like", Ramiz said with an angry voice and kicking the whole grills we had set around the fire.

-"Yeah! You can, I saw you in that island poor man. You were going to pass away!", laughing I said.

Hearing this Ramiz attacked me and after hitting each other I hit him ground, Reza and Hakan attacked me, they wanted to hit me when a shot made all of us turned stone. Angela was strongly irritated, she pointed the gun to Ramiz and his friends and said "Ramiz is right, here is a far distant free island, and everybody can do whatever he wants, now do whatever you like, then I will show you what I can do".

Jim gave me a hand to stand up, I took the gun from Angela and told her to pack all our stuff into the raft. She went into the cave and took everything, even the fishing lance.

-"Shit! Leave the lance at least", seeing there was nothing in the cave Reza said.

-"Make one if you can", Angela said.

- "My friends, don't be upset. We can make whatever we need", Ramiz said with a grin to hide his irritation.

I and Angela got on the raft and waited for others to decide. Jim did not understand us, but said some swear words to Ramiz in English and came to stand by us. Demet was by the cave entrance talking to Hakan to change his mind and join us, but clearly he was in doubt for any decision. We were all looking at Hakan. Ramiz never wanted to lose his friend so he said loudly "Hakan! Stay with us if you are a man!". Hearing this Hakan left Demet's hands and joined his friends. Demet shook her head for her sorrow. She joined us on the raft and said "Let's go, he is still stupid". I started paddling and we moved away slowly from there. Ramiz had put his hands on Reza and Hakan's shoulders and was swearing us. Reza was very irritated and shouted "Go hell with those two girls and that old man, you coward! I hope sharks cut you into pieces". I was sorry to see how unfair my friends were, the friends whom I had worked with for many years. We had passed around half a mile, but they were still swearing us. I was paddling with no care of them. Angela was really angry and said "I have to make them shut up", then she took the gun and pulled the trigger, she shot towards them. Ramiz and his friends did not expect this reaction so they jumped on the ground immediately and crouched into the cave. It was a humorous scene and we all laughed a lot.

We paddled to the north as we wanted to go to the east part of the island and find a place for living. Angela had sat beside Demet, they were talking and laughing loudly. Jim was an old man, but he was paddling as I was. I asked him about his family. His wife's name was Shargeh who had moved to the United States about thirty years before and had married him there. They had a daughter. Her name was Sarah. His wife had a heart problem and Jim believed if she heard the plane crash, she would have a heart attack. He was crying while talking about his family. I wanted to change the topic, so told the girls "Hey you! Aren't you tired of all these talking and laughing?".

-"If you know the matter you will laugh too", Angela said.

Jim was tired, I took the paddle from him. At that moment I remembered the marvelous song of " The Volga River Sailor", I was murmuring it, I had a great feeling.

- "You will lose your life with all your sacrificing. Let me help you!", Angela said, taking one of the paddles.

-"What were you laughing for?", I asked.

- "It was about Ramiz. I told Demet they had a devil's plan for you and now they have failed. They maybe attack at night to kidnap you". She laughed again and said "Imagine Ramiz comes while limping and puts Demet on his shoulder to take". I laughed too.

Demet got it that we were talking about her and said "Damn! Loose-mouth!", and we laughed again.

It was around noon when we arrived in the bay and its beauty was in front of our eyes. Apparently Jim was so excited that he stood up and put his hands on his head saying some words in English that I could not understand.

- "Why did not you live here since the first day? Here is very beautiful. If one lives here, he will never care the world", Demet asked.

-"Here is a good place, but we have not gone around the island, maybe there are better places", I said.

We reached the shallow part, seeing the clear water Angela was very excited, she gave me her paddle, took off her cloth and said "I am going to swim, do you like to join me?". I was not in the mood of swimming and shook my head. She did not care it and said "Okay!". Then she jumped into the water and started swimming around the raft. She was a skillful swimmer and sometimes was splashing water to us trying to motivate me to join. When she got that I did not have any idea she said "Remind me to teach you swimming", then she started backstroke around the raft. She was upstanding.

Arriving the beach Jim began to carry the stuff to the land. Demet had sat all the time on the raft and her legs were numb.

- "Yashar! Would you please help me?", she said, looking at me.

I hugged her to carry to the land. A little bit later Angela came out of the water with a frown and went to put on her clothes.

- "Here is a great place, if you agree we should stay here up to find a better point", Demet said.

Jim and I agreed and looked at Angela, but she put on her cloths and went to sit under a tree without any words. I thought she was angry with me as I had rejected her invitation for swimming.

-"Three positive votes and one abstained, so here was accepted", Demet said.

I gave my lighter to Jim to make a fire, then I took up one of the guns to hunt something. Angela was still looking at me with a frown and without any words she stood up and started the way of the forest. I followed her.

-"You men are all the same", on our way she began to talk and said

- "What do you mean?", I asked.

-"Don't say so! When you see a pretty woman you lose your mind", she said.

- "But you are pretty too", I said.

- "But not as pretty as Demet", she said.

- "What are you talking about? Tell everything clearly", I said.

She paused a little and said "why did you hug her to the land, didn't she come herself?".

-"Her legs were numb and she could not walk", I said.

- "She lied, she winked me in your hug, wanted to make me annoyed", she replied.

I got it that they had a jealous feeling. I shook my head and went on my way. A few steps later she came and took my hand quietly.

- "Tell me what there is in your mind", I said.

"Well, when I saw you for the first time I thought you are the man of my dreams. I know you are married, but now everybody thinks.....", she smiled and said.

I put my hand on her mouth, when she was silent I said "So you know I am married! I have said several times that I am going to leave this damn island, so put an end to this topic, I don't want to hear even one word." I looked down and said "Angela, please, I love my wife and son!".

When I looked at her I saw she had burst into tears, but I continued my way without caring her tears. During some hours that we were together Angela did not talk anymore. It was clear my words had put their effects and I hoped she forgot this love. It was noon when we came back with some hunted birds and some fruits. Our friends were waiting for us under a tree. I passed the hunts to Jim to make lunch and I went to take a rest under a tree.

After lunch I wanted to smoke. There were just a few cigarettes.

" What should we do right now?", Jim asked.

I lit my cigarette and asked "Imagine you are going to stay in this island for a two month holiday with these things you have. What are you doing?".

-"Before everything we should make a shelter", Demet said.

- "Tomorrow we go to the forest and bring bamboo to make a house in a few days, a house with two or three rooms", Jim said.

-"What are you doing after making the house?", I asked.

"After shelter, we have the problem of food. I don't know anything else", looking at Angela, Demet said.

"Where are you going to prepare fresh water if it is not going to rain for a few days? I mean we should think of making dishes to save fresh water", I said.

I puffed off my cigarette and went on, "they are the necessities, then after we should think of a good alternative for shampoo, soap, toothbrush and toothpaste. We should have some things for our free times too; of course, according to our condition, we should think of sending signals to ships and airplanes. And if our holiday lasts more than two months, our most important job will be finding a way to leave the island".

Everybody was thinking. Angela was silent up to that moment, but suddenly she said "I know some plants we can use to wash our hair and teeth. We can make soap by mixing melted oil and ash. To save water for drinking we can use bamboo for making barrels, we can make even spoons, forks and plates with bamboo too. We can use bamboo tissues to make spectacra and tennis balls. We can make a hammock and hang it from these coconut trees to take a rest and enjoy these beautiful scenes. We can make mats to cover the floor and the walls of the rooms. There are many herbs here too".

Finishing her talking, she looked at me meaningfully and then looked down. I thought she wanted me to understand that if we wanted to live on the island we would have needed her a lot. Angela had affected Jim and Demet. They were very excited.

- "What should we do with your friends?", Jim asked me.

- "We should leave them alone for a while. Whenever we see they are regretful we bring them here", I said.

-"And if they don't feel regretful?", Demet asked.

-"Then they will stay here forever and enjoy themselves", I said sorrowfully.

That day I had paddled a lot, so I preferred to take a rest for the rest of the day. I had just a few cigarettes and I did not know what to do then. If I had not annoyed Angela, I could ask her to find something alternative. I sat beside a tree looking at the sea, I was smoking and thinking about my friends. I thought I should leave at least one of the guns and fishing lances for them. That night Demet was singing with her fantastic voice to the others, but I was not in a good mood and I was thinking about the adventurous days we surely would have in the future.

S annoyance ` Ramiz

Tomorrow morning Angela and Jim had already wakened up and had made the breakfast ready. Demet was still sleeping. I went by the sea to wash my face, Jim stood beside me and while he was doing exercise he said "today will be a full working day. Be sure I will work like a bull". We started our way at eight. Before going I gave one of the guns to Demet and said "take care of you. If there is a danger, don't fear, just shoot even if the danger is from my friends". After the event of the yesterday I was not sore at Angela and I wanted to leave her alone for a while. She had noticed my mind, so she did not say anything and just stood to watch us moving away.

Half an hour later we arrived in bamboo jungle. I was cutting the bamboos with the sword and Jim was cutting their branches and leaves. It was around one hour we were working when suddenly we heard a shot. I thought there was a danger for the girls so I asked Jim to stay there and go on the work and I came back to see what had happened. As he had a bad experience of being alone in the jungle, he wanted to come with me, but I put my hand on his shoulder and said "a bull never fears especially when he has a sword in his hand. You are strong'. "I will try", he said while smiling. I took up the gun and started running. When I arrived at the beach I saw the girls sitting beside a tree. I had run a long way, with a trembling voice I called Demet. I was behind Angela. Before she knew my voice she took the gun and shot. I was lucky as she lost her balance and could not shoot me. When she got her mistake she ran towards me, hugged me and while crying she said some things in her mother tongue. I cleaned her tears, but she was continually saying "Oh darling! Please forgive me, I did not know your voice". She had been frightened by something.

When she was quiet, she said "I was swimming when I heard Demet was screaming. I attached her quickly. She was really afraid of and pointed something behind one of the trees. Somebody was there, then I took up the gun and warned him to come back, but he did not listen and I had to shoot him". Then, while she was crying, she put her head on my chest and said "Yashar, it was Ramiz, I think I hurt his arm. What will happen if his wound is bad?". I consulate her and said "tomorrow we should go and see him, you will help if there is a problem". Demet was pale and her hands were trembling. She was frightened and wanted me not to leave them alone. I preferred to stay with Demet and Angela should join Jim. She was satisfied not for my suggestion, but as I had talked to and hugged her. She was a perfect opportunist. I gave Demet some fruits to feel okay up to Angela and Jim's arrival.

- "This is a strange girl. Whatever she said yesterday was going to become true. Ramiz was going to kidnap me", she said after a while.

-"Don't worry. Nobody can hurt you. And I don't think Ramiz had come here to make a problem for you. Maybe they like making somebody fun of but they are not lewd", I said.

- "Why did he come here then?", she asked.

- "Maybe he wanted to steal our stuff. Perhaps it was just for curiosity", I replied.

-"If they are not bad, why did we leave them?", she asked.

-"As I don't want they insult you and we proceed our works as we have planned", I said.

A little later Angela and Jim joined us with some of the bamboos. It was cloudy. We made a shelter immediately and covered it with leaves and branches. When we carried our stuff inside the shelter it started to rain, so heavily that it could turn a desert into a green jungle in one hour. That night we drank enough water. Jim was very tired and was massaging his legs and arms. I felt compassion for him. He was smiling, but he was really tired so he said good night and went to sleep by the fire. Demet was still worried of the evening event.

-Looking out of the shelter she came closer and said "Do you think they come at midnight?".

I laughed and said "in this rainy weather? And due to Angela's shooting, I think they never dare to come even one mile around here. Feel free".

- "What is the plan for tomorrow?", she asked again.

-"Angela and I will go to see Ramiz, we should bring some things for them too. You stay here", I replied.

- "But I am fearful", she said.

-"Jim stays with you. And you have a gun too, so why do you fear?", I replied.

Angela had stood by the shelter and looking outside. She was silent up to that moment, but she said suddenly, "what do you mean we are taking some things for them? Do you want to improve their behavior by kindness? I think we should leave Ramiz to die". Then she touched her hair and said "I wish I had pointed his head".

It made me upset. Putting wood on the fire I said "You are a doctor! Instead of thinking his healthy, did you feel regretful why you have not killed him? How do you know, maybe he was hungry and came here".

Angela had nothing to say, she looked at me, shook her head and saying some things in her mother tongue, she came beside the fire to dry her hair. That night Demet slept beside Angela. Demet was screaming at midnight due to the nightmare, made us to wake up suddenly several times.

Early in the morning Angela wakened me up to go to the jungle for food. It was sunny and the colorful birds were singing. When we arrived at the forest Angela took my arms and before I could do anything she kissed me. It was completely unexpected. I did not like her act, but I admit that she made me feel something strange. Before I could say something, she put her hand on my mouth and said "excuse me for my stupid words". Then she took a deep breath and said "I love you so much that even if you want to forget me, I will go on until you give a positive reply for my marriage offer".

I shook my head and said "Marriage offer! I am really sorry for you. How many times I should say that I am married, I have a wife and a son and I will come back to join them".

-"And what if we cannot leave the island forever?", she asked.

-"Let me tell you something. Even if we have to live here forever, I will never get married to a crazy girl like you?", I said.

Her speaking was very strange for me. This was the first time I had faced a person and she loved me so much. I had never seen this behavior and never heard these words, even from my wife. Angela had really fallen in love with me, she was adoring me. I was sure I could not change her mind, but as I wanted to tell her my decision I frowned and said " if once more you want to talk about love, I will take up my stuff and leave all you. Be sure I will do so!". Then I continued my way with no care of her feelings.

All the time we were in the jungle I did not talk to Angela but I could see how innocent she was looking at me and wanted to talk to. She was picking up some herbs and putting them in her pocket. I guessed she was going to make a balm for Ramiz's hand, but as I did not want to talk to her I did not ask about them too.

When we arrived at the beach Demet and Jim had already woken up. After the breakfast, I gave one of the guns to Jim and said "I trust you. Take care of yourselves". Then I went closer and asked "Do you know how to use the gun?". He brought his head closer "Be sure! I remember some things from the Vietnam war". I was astonished, Jim was so quiet and self-contained that I never thought he could do the fighting. Anybody in his shoes tried to describe his memories of war with honor and pride, but he had such a great personality. He got a great character in my mind and I felt myself so little that I pressed his hands and said "Goodbye commander!". I packed all the things we were going to take on the raft and started the way with Angela. Waving hands by the sea Demet said " Come back soon. We will wait you for the lunch". Along the way I was very excited to get familiar with an old soldier of the Vietnam War. I was paddling with full energy. He was a symbol of resistance and I knew that he had lots of experiences, useful for living on that island.

The sea was quiet and it was one hour I was paddling. Angela had never talked to me up to that moment, but suddenly she broke the silence and said "Why are you going to give them these bamboos?". I had a glance at her and kept on paddling. She had noticed my careless behavior, got one of the paddles and started. Again she began to talk and asked "What do you think of the boys' reaction when they see us?".

I had never thought of this matter. "I don't know", I replied carelessly.

-"If attack us?", again she asked.

I thought if they wanted to insult me, I would control myself; but if they wanted to insult Angela, I would have a strong reaction especially as I had a gun.

We arrived at the cave entrance. Everywhere was quiet, nobody was at the beach. I called them, but there was no reply. We entered the cave, everywhere was dirty and in a mess.

- "Oh Angela! They did not know your kindness", seeing the cave Angela said.

We heard a cough. Ramiz had laid by the fire at one corner of the cave. Seeing us, he wanted to sit down. He had wrapped his hand with a piece of cloth and it was clear that he was not in a bad condition. When he saw us he turned his face and said with irritation "Why have you come? Do you want to see we have died of starvation?".

-"You stupid! We have brought you some food. Actually, we cared you", I said.

- "We don't need your compassion, be sure we can run this life", he said.

-"It is clear!", I said.

-" What is wrong with us?", he asked with astonishment.

I stared at him and said "why did you come to our lodge? Surely you wanted to steal something. Poor Demet, she was very frightened".

With a serious look he said "No! Why stealing. I was just curious, I did not want to make anybody frightened".

Angela did not like Ramiz and was looking at him with a frown, but she went closer to check his hand. Ramiz passed his hand back.

-"Don't be silly! She is a doctor and she just wants to visit you", I said.

Angela began to do her work, and I went to bring food from the raft. I saw Reza and Hakan in a far distant jumping in the water, it was clear they were busy fishing. I carried all the stuff into the cave. Seeing the bamboos Ramiz was very astonished and asked "What are these bamboos for?".

-"For hitting you", I said.

He thought I was serious, so he was really shocked. I told Angela "take the bigger one and hit him as much as you can, I go to see the others". Angela was crazy of frightening, so she took up a bamboo quickly and stood beside Ramiz and said "You were taking a peep at us, I will show you!". Ramiz thought we were serious, so he shouted "Wait! Wait! I promise never to do it again". Hearing this Angela and I started laughing.

-"Crazy! If we wanted to hit you why we came for your visiting", I told Ramiz.

When he got the point, he turned his face and mumbled "Mean!".

- "The east part of the island is full of bamboo, you can make what you need", I told him.

He thought a while and said, "But we have nothing to cut".

- "When we finish our job I can lend you the sword for a few days, of course, if you put an end to your wicked behavior", I said.

Angela had finished her work "the wound is not too bad, I put balm on it, it will be okay in a week, but you should not touch water to avoid infection".

When we wanted to come out of the cave we faced Reza and Hakan. Reza started to swear. I was angry, but I did not say anything and just looked at him. My silence made him more irritated and he began vulgarity, I lost my control and punched him on his chin and he fell down. Hakan jumped over me and took my hands, Reza wanted to attack me that suddenly Angela took up the gun and shot to the cave ceiling. It was such a harsh sound that I could not hear anything for a few minutes. Reza and Hakan did not expect such a reaction from Angela and had been shocked.

-"Let him free you villains or I will shoot you", she shouted.

Hakan quit the attack by a gesture from Ramiz. Angela was like a wounded tiger and said with irritation "You are really poor, do you think I could not kill Ramiz yesterday; I could, but I did not as of your friendship with Yashar. You are really rude. If one more time you want to come to our area I will shoot your head, try it if you dare". Then she took the hunted birds we had brought and said "Let's go. An idiot man should die of starvation". Leaving the cave she told Reza "Do you know what mistake Yahsar did? He saved idiot men like you and your rude friends!".

Coming back, I was really irritated. I was thinking why Reza, my colleague, the man I had saved him, had been changed so much and forgotten my kindness. I was sure I would have killed anybody else if he had behaved me like this. I had a bad feeling, I was going to burst of irritation. I had got red. I broke out in a cold sweat. My heart was beating fast. Angela had got my bad feeling so she took the paddles and said something with astonishment, but at that moment I could not hear anything except my heart beating. I could not stand anymore, so I took off my clothes and jumped into the water, I was swimming like a crazy man to feel free of the bad feeling inside me. A little later Angela jumped into the water too, she attached me, touched my face and said "Darling! Don't make disturb yourself. I am always with you, nobody can hurt you", and she kissed me. Her kiss was so enjoyable that I lost my control and hugged her. At that moment I could not feel anything except her warm and soft body and I was just kissing her.

An hour later we had sat on the raft eating fruit. The raft was moved with the rhythm of the waves and Angela was serving me with fruits without any talking. She had stared me and I felt she wanted me to accept that she had made me fall in love with her. I smiled and said "thanks for your help. I will never forget it", but she said nothing and just smiled and nodded her head. We had arrived near the bay and I knew that Jim and Demet were waiting us for lunch, so I started to paddle.

We arrived at the beach. Demet was busy cooking, grilled fish smell had made me feel so hungry that I could eat a whale. A few minutes later, Jim came back from hunting. I was very happy to see him again. His presence on the island made me hopeful, especially when I knew that he had war experience for years. During the food Demet was describing all difficulties she had in catching fish and crab with her wounded leg and the others were laughing but I was just thinking Angela. She looked at me a few times and smiled, but I felt just regretful about one thing. I wished my wife had loved me as much as Angela.

Build the camp

That day I was so tired that I could not do anything else, so lying down under a tree I took a rest and saved energy for tomorrow. I was going to make a house with a few rooms for our living and it involved to bring lots of bamboo to the beach. I was going to make a wall around the house to keep it safe from wind, wild animals, and my wicked friends' attack. I was estimating how much bamboo we would need and how long it would take to make the house if Jim and the girls would help while we would have to stop the work on rainy days, and I got it that it we needed two months. I was busy of thinking and did not know when I had slept. I was sleeping when I heard a desirable voice saying "Darling! Get up". I opened my eyes. Angela was beside me eating fruit. Jim and Demet were repairing the roof of the shelter.

Eating a piece of Papaya, Angela said "It is delicious, take a piece!". She was eating with a great appetite that I felt hungry.

-"You slept well", cleaning her mouth, she said.

- "How many hours?", I asked.

- "Two hours", she said smiling.

Jim and Demet joined us too. Demet took a piece of the fruit and with a naughty smile said "A great private chat!".

- "I think we should start making the house tomorrow. I see we would have to stay here for a long time", Jim said.

- "So tomorrow all of us should go to the forest to bring bamboo", Angela said.

-"Not the girls! You should control the sea everyday over the northern rocks. If you see something, you will signal with fire and gun shooting", I said.

Jim stood up, taking off his shirt, he said "I am going to swim, do you like to join?". I was tired, so I said no. Hearing the word "swimming" Angela was astonished and said "Oh man! He was swimming like a motor boat". Then she started to exaggerate my swimming to Demet, she even told her that if I had raced with a shark I would have wined. Demet had believed her, so she said "I am not good at swimming. Can you teach me?". Angela was jealous so before I could reply Demet she frowned and said "No need. Swimming trainer for ladies should be a woman. I can swim as well as Yashar. I will teach you". We all laughed.

From the next day we began to bring bamboo and make the house. Every day morning Jim and I were going to the east part of the island to cut the bamboo and carry them to the beach. As we had planned the girls were controlling around the island over the northern rocks with the binoculars. It was getting hotter and more humid, but we were to stand it and keep on the work. The only thing bothered me was the insect bites. Once I got such a big insect bite that if Angela had not helped I would have surely died. Angela was an eastern girl with so many skills. Every day she went over the rocks with some leaves and trees thin branches and in the evening she made us surprised with a new thing she had made. She had made many things: hat, spoons, forks, hammock mat, bucket, even barrels to save rainwater. She was like a magic box where one could find everything. As Jim believed if she had the technology she could make an intercontinental rocket with bamboo too. I could admit that there were three things made the life easier on the island: sword, bamboo, and Angela. She was really skillful.

Whenever we were appreciating her skills, she was taking a pose saying " Needed for all houses!".

Due to raining for a long time, the camp took one week more to be completed. During all the nine weeks we were busy making the camp, I was just thinking to finish the work as soon as possible. I was unaware my friends. All the days I was so tired that I couldn't stay awake after dinner, I was sleeping beside the fire, I did not care that Angela was sleeping in my arms until mornings.

The first work in making the camp was to get a piece of land up a small hill towards the bay. Then we fenced a wall around the circle land by the bamboos and made a robust gate for it. Then it was the turn of the rooms. To respect Jim we started to make his room first. We made a bower in the middle of the land to spend some hours together during the day. The room floor was a little bit higher than the ground to provide a stony stove for cooking and keeping the room warm. The stove had been surrounded by the bamboos to keep the fire on against the wind blowing and being expanded around. Each room had two windows, one at the back and the other towards the other rooms. Making the windows I selected the length to the width equals to one to six that are "golden numbers", it was a secret and my friends did not know anything about it. Once I had read in a book that Leonardo Dawinchi had used these numbers a lot in his picture "The Last Supper", to paint the windows in the picture that made them fabulous, the secret of the art work beauty, the one that just a few people had noticed. Beside we furnished the room with a hammock, a table and a chair, a bed and a shelf. Of course, as Angela had asked me, I made my bed and hers a little bit bigger than others. We covered the ceilings with dunnage, so compacted that even a drop of water could not penetrate the room. Finally, we made a public toilet and a bathroom. We were amateurs in making a house, but it was so strong that looked as if we had years of experience in making structures. Completing each of the rooms, Angela was standing in the front door and saying some words in her mother tongue like the wizards to take away the mishap from the area. Of course she then admitted she had said some   gossips. Then we were making a wretch of beautiful flowers, putting it on the head of the owner of the room, we were dancing like the Indians, carrying the owner of the room to the room belonged, we were singing with strange sounds. We were enjoying the whole night and the room owner was making a delicious food to welcome us. The last room was mine. After a good ceremony for opening it Demet said "I think we should have a name for our camp. What is your idea?".

- "You are right, but what?", Angela said.

They all looked at me that meant I should name the camp. I thought a little and then asked their permission to call it by the name of my hometown, "Lachin camp". They all agreed and we decided to engrave it at the first time on the top of the entrance. Jim wanted to talk a little, he coughed and said "I am not good at lecturing, but I have not made a mistake in joining you. I thank you so much for all the works you have done for us and I am honored to have a friend like you". He breathed deeply and said "we all owe you this comfort and joy, if my friends let, I am going to give you the honor of the camp managing the same as Americans do".

He then took a wooden key out of his cloth and delivered to me. I was so happy that I felt I had got the honored doctorate from Oxford University. I was so happy that couldn't help me of crying and hugged Jim. Angela and Demet joined us and hugging me they thanked. That night I had a strange feeling. On the one hand, I was happy of my new friends' thanks; and on the other hand, I was upset by my old friends' behavior and how they had not appreciated my help.

That night it was late when all left my room and I was cleaning it up, the door was opened and Angela came in. She had taken off her clothes and was looking like a beautiful mermaid under the moonlight. Without saying anything she laid down on my bed with coquetry, and asked me to join her. I had got used to sleep with her since we had started to make the camp, so I laid down beside her without any words. That night the moon was a complete circle and it was making our sleep a dreamy one. Touching my hair, she kissed me and said "my dear, I adore you so much that I wished to have all the beauties deliver to you. Your love is so holy that I think the sky and the earth move around just for your sake. I'd like to bring all stars, the moon and the sun for you. You are the soul of my life and I live for you. My life is for you, take it". After that night I had changed my idea towards Angela in a way that she belonged to me. I rarely thought of my family and wherever I was going she was following me. I had fallen in her love, though I could never admit it.

Unwelcome guest

A few days later, Jim and I were sitting under the pergola, talking about a design for a big sailing boat. The girls were making lunch while suddenly Demet screamed loudly and run towards us and before we could do anything Angela picked up the gun and shoot into the air, stepped towards the gate and shouted "Show yourself or I will kill you". Soon after a cloth tied to a piece of wood came out behind the wall. Then a man with a dirty, torn cloth and long hair was appeared. We did not know him at first, but looking carefully we saw Hakan. He had come to meet us. It was undesirable to see him in that position. He felt ashamed and looked down in silence. I took his hand and we all went to sit under the pergola. His appearance was wretched with a long mustache and beard and dirty tangled hair. Looking at Hakan, Jim touched his shaved face and smiled me, I knew he wanted to thank me for the shaving stuff I had with myself. Angela served Hakan with juice. He looked very thirsty. Drinking the juice he was looking at us and the camp with a surprise as if he had come from another planet. Everything was new for him. Drinking another glass he felt fresh and said "since you have left us our life has been like the primitive man's life, we have eaten fruit and raw fish, we have forgotten food tastes. Ramiz is just eating, sleeping and ordering. No order there is and we quarrel on food sometimes. They behave me like a slave and when they knew I wanted to join you they hit me and threatened to kill me". Demet had believed his words and was crying so Hakan tried to affect her feelings. Of course he was not completely true and they could never behave him in that way, but he had been bored of that life and wanted us to let him a room in the camp. He finished his words and looked at us, when he saw they looked at me he turned me and waited for my decision. I was in doubt to accept him or reject away.

- "Don't you think of a trick?", Jim whispered me.

- "What a trick?", I asked.

- "I don't know, may be ridiculous, but we had so many stories like this in Vietnam", he said.

 - "Any suggestion?", I asked him.

- "I don't feel good to him, if they had bothered him as he said, he must have left them earlier than", he said.

   I thought for a while and accepted his logic. I said, "Of course, this is just a guess, I think he should be under inspection for a while".

That day we talked to Hakan for a long time and explained him all the regulations of the camp. We decided he would stay for a few days and reminded him that if everything was okay, he could make a room for himself in the camp area. Although I am a pessimistic man, Jim's words made me worried, so I asked Angela to watch all Hakan's works without saying anything about it to Demet or Jim. That day, Hakan took a bath and shaved. To celebrate his joining us, we had a big meal that night. During the supper we were all talking and laughing, Hakan was unaware that all his movements were under control. The party lasted until midnight, I felt sleepy so I said good night to everybody and went to my room. It was decided that Hakan should sleep in Demet's room. Due to Jim's view about Hakan, I was a little worried and could not sleep well, I feared that he would open the gate to his friends and they would damage our camp. I was awake for two hours, but then I felt sleepy and went to bed. I was sleeping while somebody tried to wake me up, I opened my eyes and saw someone beside my bed, and I thought it was Hakan so I wanted to jump over him but it was Angela. She said Hakan was busy checking out the rooms and getting our stuffs. I asked her to stay in my bed and I took the Samurai sword and went out of the window. Hakan had thought we were all sleeping, so he had gone into the rooms and had taken whatever he thought would be useful. Taking up the guns he smiled happily and went towards the gate. I had got the sword in my hand and had stood in a dark place. When he went closer to the gate, I coughed and he took one of the guns over his shoulder quickly and looked around. I went a few steps forward, so he could see me under the moonlight, he was shocked to see me, he shouted with an angry voice "let me go or……".

- "Or what?", I said.

- "Yashar, I don't want to shoot, don't make me to do so", he said.

I laughed so loudly that the others got out of bed and came to the gate. Hakan had been surrounded by us, he was very frightened that moving around him and threatened to shoot, but I was still laughing.

- "Crazy! I am serious, if you don't let me go, I will shoot", getting angry he shouted.

- "Do it if you dare!", I said.

He pressed his teeth together and said "You want this", and he triggered. For one moment everybody was frightened and Angela shouted, but nothing was shot. He was completely confused, again and again, he triggered, but it was useless. "Hey boy! A gun never shoots without a breech block", I said with laughing. He did not know I had taken the breech block of the guns before going to bed. Suddenly Angela hit him on his head with a bamboo and he fell down.

The next morning we were all gathered under the pergola to punish Hakan. We tied his hands and feet to a tree, it was clear he still had the headache. My friends were angry with him and we decided to give our vote for his punishment. Angela stood up and said "these islands belong to Indonesia and he should be punished according to hard regulations of my country. In my country to punish a traitor there was a very harsh action and that is they take the guilty man up a rock and then cut his hands and feet alive and throw them for the sharks". Demat and Jim had believed her and it was clear on their faces that they had not agreed with this idea. Of course I knew Angela, what she said was a false story as she liked to frighten people, she had exaggerated in this case too. Hakan was going to have a heart attack with her words, especially when Angela was speaking with a frown and looking at Hakan with irritation. Demat suggested that we should tie his hands and feet and threw him into the sea; if he died, that was okay and if he could save himself we should make him free. Jim had lots of war experience and suggested to have a military trial for him and shoot him. Everybody was waiting to hear my idea. I paused a little and said "I think we should tear off his shirt and tie his hands on back and release him to come back to his friends". They all disagreed with me at first, but finally they accepted my idea and we did it so. He went a few steps, then stood and thanked us and left the camp while he was crying. Demat was unhappy with this punishment so she told me "What a harsh punishment! I think he will never forget it while he is alive, he will laugh at us." Interrupting her words, Angela said "Hey! Care your words. I don't know why Yashar had such an idea, but I am sure it was the best punishment". Angela was right as the punishment looked simple, but it was the hardest one. To join his friends he had to pass the dense forest on his way and I was sure he would be injured by trees leaf and branches with no cloth, the one which would take lots of time to be cured. I did not want him to lose his life for a small robbery, I just wanted to punish him to be aware of his nasty work and to be treated.

After this event, I decided to improve the camp's safety, that day we had just two guns and three cartridges; we were weak against any attack. I was sure Hakan would tell the whole of the story to his friends and I feared they got temptation to attack us with a previous plan. So I talked to Jim to go to the crashed plane to bring some guns and ammunitions to the camp. When we were leaving the camp in the morning I gave the guns to Angela and asked her to take care of the camp and Demet, I wanted to come back until the evening but saying goodbye I had a bad feeling and never wanted to leave Angela.

On the way I told Jim the whole story of finding out the Japanese plane, he was listening with eager and I felt he was stepping quickly to see the crashed plane as soon as possible. It was getting cloudy and I wanted to get into the plane before the rain but it started early. It was thundering and Jim was cutting the tree branches with the sword to pave the way. I was following him with a strange feeling of a Vietnam forest in the Second World War. I was so excited that I was feeling all of a sudden some almond-shaped short soldiers would attack us with their bayonets, I knew it was just a false feeling but I was looking around carefully. When we arrived by the crashed plane Jim stopped and stared at it with astonishment. I knew he was reviewing the war stories, so I took his hand to enter the plane. Jim was taking everything, looking at it carefully, then retelling the war memories, bad memories of killing, burning, and displacing innocent people. Seeing a grenade he started crying so that I could not control myself and I burst into tears. While crying, he said "God damn me, I am a sinner". Then he added, "During the war when we arrived in a village we burned everywhere due to fear of "Viet Kongs", we were throwing grenades to every hole. I burnt a house and killed the residents, then found a ground stove and felt somebody was there, so I threw a grenade into it quickly. After the explosion I saw there were three kids less than ten years old, hiding there because of fear but they had been killed brutally. I was getting crazy. I had killed hundreds of people, but it was not important for me as I had accepted it as a holy war, but that day I killed three innocent children cruelly". Jim cried the whole day and I did not remember when I had fallen asleep.

When I got up in the morning it was still raining, Jim was sleeping. It was a little cold and I was hungry, so I took up one of the guns and left the plane to find food and wood. It was still raining and the earth was totally muddy, making hard to walk. A few steps from the plane, I heard a sound from the bushes, I pulled the breech block and pointed the gun towards them. I stepped forward quietly and pushed away the bushes by the gun. It was unbelievable, there I saw some white woolly goats, pasturing under the rain. I wondered how they had come to the island. Had anybody brought them there? I had many questions without answers but I was sure of one thing; that there were so many things on the island that we should see.

Since I had arrived in the island I had not eaten red meat, I had forgotten its taste; but I could not shoot them, so I put aside the gun and wanted to catch one of them. They were faster than me and as the ground were wet and slippery I had been completely muddy. I tried again and again, but it was useless. I was so tired that I decided to sit down under a tree to find a way. I remembered my childhood when we were going to the village we normally used to get the mother goat, then the baby goats were following their mother. This trick did it work and after half an hour a group of ten baby goats and their mother were near the plane. Seeing the goats, Jim laughed happily and I was glad to make him feel happy after the last night upsetting event. Due to the continuous raining, we sat by the fire the whole day and drank goat milk.

The next morning when I got up it was sunny. The smell of wet woods of the night fire was pleasant. I got up and looked at the goats. They were all healthy and were pasturing by the plane. The birds were singing and the golden rays of the sun were everywhere, it was the time of packing our stuff and coming back to the camp. I hope Angela was good after these few days. Due to the goats, Jim got up too, and came out of the plane. He got one of the goats and started to touch and talk to it. I remembered my son who was beyond his father's touching and talking to. It was the time to do something. I decided to make ready all I needed for a big journey and see my family again.

I entered the plane and took all the weapons, including four guns, three boxes of bullets and some grenades to feel free of probable attacks by my friends. Jim was touching the goats; when he saw me with all those weapons, he said "if it is not enough I should take some too". I laughed and said "the rest are for the friends" and we started the way.

I was going forward and Jim was following me with the goat in his arms, a few steps farther the other goats were coming slowly. The stuff I was carrying was very heavy and it was very difficult for me to walk in the forest, but I did not want to make Jim stressful and did not ask his help. Despite of all difficulties we arrived in the camp around noon. Angela had sat near the gate and seeing us, she ran towards. She was very happy to see us, seems she had been far from me for so many years, her beautiful hair was moving in the air so desirable that I felt it was happy too. Attaching us she hugged me and started to cry due to her happiness. I kissed her head and said "Don't cry, I am here beside you". She cleaned her tears and said " These days far from you were very hard. Yashar I will die without you, promise to take me with you wherever you go". I touched her face and said "I promise". Hearing this promise she smiled. Meanwhile, Jim attached, seeing all these goats Angela was jumping like kids.

-"Yashar, do you know what these goats bring us?", she asked.

- "At least we will not have calcium deficiency", I replied.

- "Oh man, you are great!", she said with a smile and kissed me again.

Since we had got friendly relations, she tried to use every opportunity to kiss me. We arrived by the gate and she pointed to a beautiful sign on top of the door saying 'Lachin Camp, enter if you have merit". I was very happy and thanked her by touching her hair.

That day there was a great excitement in the camp, Jim and I took a bath and sat under the bower. We were looking at the girls running to catch the goats. Their hitting the ground was very interesting and we laughed a lot. We made them ridiculous so much that they forgot the goats and started to throw us mud and sludge, we had no choice except running, but we hit the ground like them and our clothes got dirty.

Pottery

After dinner we were all under the bower and as usual everybody wanted to suggest a topic for talking. Demet believed that we should make a barn for the goats. Angela had the best plan and we all accepted that. Jim talked about making candles for making all the room. I remembered a program on Iran television showing how the local fishermen catch a shark and use its oil to grease their wooden ships body. I explained to my friends that how we could stand on the northern rocks of the bay and hunt the sharks, but the only problem was that we had no dish to melt the fats. Hearing this point Angela thought for a while and said "I know it!", and she ran to her room. We were all confused of her works. A little while she came back with some clay and put it on the table. She put her hands on the table and asked "I think we can solve the problem with this".

-"What is this?", Demat asked.

-"Clay, when Yahsar and Jim went, I felt depressed, I went out of the camp and sat down the hill. I was busy with the soil then I found that it was clay, I wanted to make a statue while Yashar was not here, and now I think that we can solve our problem with that", Angela said.

It was an interesting idea and we all accepted it. We decided to start making clay dishes and whatever we needed for the day after. But it was a hard work to make all the dishes we wanted and we needed a furnace to cook them as well. Angela and Jim's offers made them so busy that they forgot I had something to say, making a ship and leaving the island.

Late at night I was thinking about making a big sailing ship and I was setting the details of the plan. Angela had laid beside me and was talking about everything. I was confirming her words to let her think that I am listening to. After a while she turned my head with her hand and asked with a surprise "hey! Do you listen to me?". I did not know what she was talking about so I said "you are right!". She got up and sat down and said "what do mean I am right? Did you know what I said?". I was not in a good mood to explain so I said "I think it is due to pass a hard day. I want to sleep if you let me". She lied down beside me again and while she was placing herself in my hug, she said "you are right, we should sleep".

- "I mean I want to sleep alone", I said.

She was astonished and said "I am sure there is something wrong with you today as you never wanted anything else instead of my arms".

-"We have made one room for everybody to take a rest there alone, not to bother others and not to let anybody bothers him", I said.

She opened her eyes and said "bothering!, do you think that I bother you? I don't think so and meanwhile these few days that you had gone I was alone and I did never feel happy".

Then she closed her eyes and said "Ok! Don't disturb me, let me sleep. Tomorrow we have lots of things to do".

I wondered what I should do with this cheeky girl. She closed her eyes and went to sleep, but I was still dreaming the ship and leaving the island.

The next morning we got up by the goats sounds, I watched out, they were in the campus eating everything they saw. I came beside the bed to wake Angela up. I woke her up and said " you used to get up earlier than me to make the breakfast, get up lazy girl!" she took my hand and pulled it. I fell down on her. She said hello and kept on " you made me lazy, before this I was sleeping alone but now I am with you. Believe me, I am calm beside you. Tell me just one word that you love me then I will get up". I stood up and said "I don't want the breakfast. Just show me the clays place". I shook my head and left the room.

Demet had started milking the goats into the dishes made with the bamboos. I drank a glass of the milk, it was so delicious that I remembered all the days of my childhood when we were taking the sheep to the pasture. Soon Jim and Angela joined us and after drinking milk we left the campus. I have never liked working with clay so I confirmed that I would not do anything there. As I knew Angela liked working with clay and she had some experience in that art, therefore I suggested that she would be the charge of the clay workshop we were going to establish. She was very excited, she was over the moon. Poor Angela, she did not know that by this idea I just wanted to be calm and take a rest without her. Within a few days we built a clay workshop equipped with a furnace. My plan had worked, I was really in calm; Angela was so interested in this work that all the day she was working there. She was getting so tired that was sleeping there without any food. I was taking her to her room and then I was free to do my works. At first she had problems to adjust the furnace and many dishes had been broken down but after a while she had made a set of dishes, she showed them to us. She was very excited that I think "Madam Couri" was never like when she discovered radium. Little by little she got much skill in clay works so she decided to draw some sketches on the dishes and colored them with some plant colors and fire ash, so pretty that were looking like antiques. Jim and Demet were encouraging her to do new things and sometimes they helped her too. But I knew what she had in her mind, to attract our attention to her art, to waste the time. She had lost all her relatives, she wanted to waste our time to forget leaving the island, the heaven she wanted to live in. Whenever I was talking about the plan for leaving the island, they had an excuse, they tried to change the topic. But it was enough to talk about making clay dishes or flying a kite then they were eager to express their ideas for a long time. They were so busy of little things that they had forgotten our main work was to find a way to rescue ourselves from that island. Sometimes I preferred to leave the talking to take a rest in my room.

All the days Angela was busy in the clay workshop, Jim and I were going to the forest to bring bamboos. We were going to make a wharf in front of the camp. The tide of that area was so much that made us to make a long wharf to have water around during the days too. It took one month, but was pleasant for me as I had practiced my childhood dream. The day it was finished, we had a simple ceremony, when Jim and Demet left there, Angela said " I wish we had a ship too, I have never seen a wharf without a ship"

-"We will start making a few ships as soon as possible" I said.

- "Why a few?", she asked with a surprise.

- "One big sail ship for carrying our stuffs and some boats for recreation", I said.

-"What do you mean?", she asked.

- "It is very clear, one big ship for those who want to leave the island and the others for those who like to stay at this island forever", I said.

She was taken aback by what I said.

- "Why are you angry? Here the life is good, we have everything we need, I am sure one day they will rescue us, until then we.....", she said.

I interrupted her words and shouted "I do not stay here, even one minute".

She had never seen me angry like that, started crying and with a trembling voice said "Don't you think that I will die if you leave me alone? Man! I live as you are here".

While she was crying, she hugged me and said "Yahsar, I have you here, your soul, your body is mine; but if you leave me, you will be for somebody else. I have made a pretty life here with you, please don't collapse it".

- "Angela! Why don't you want to understand, I love somebody else, I have forgotten my son's face. Do you understand me?", I said.

She ran towards the camp while she was crying. That night the full moon was in the sky. I sat down on the wharf and watching the pretty moon and recalling the family memories I cried. That night I decided not to talk about leaving the island anymore and start making a ship in a good time with nobody's help.

Shark hunting

After a hard work for one month the dishes for melting shark oil were prepared so we decided to go hunting. The day before set up, we put three layers of bamboo on the Braque and tied them to save it against probable attacks of the sharks. It was the hunting day, we were all stressful except Demet, and she did not know swimming so she had to stay in the camp to take care of the goats. We had planned to climb on the rocks and pour a bird's blood in the water and then wait for the sharks. I had heard that sharks are good at smelling and can smell blood from twenty kilometers. We had decided to hunt a few sharks, tie them to the Braque and come back to the coast. We had to be very careful of the injured shark. The hardest part of the work was jumping into the sea to tie the rope to the sharks' tails; that was my duty. We had added some extra layers of bamboo to the Braque and it was overweight, but we were so stressful that we were sculling in silence. Angela had sat in front of the Braque and to start the work she took the dead bird we had hunted yesterday in her hand and said "Poor bird! Never thought to be bait for sharks". Then she started to make bird sounds and said "do you know what it said? I know the birds' language on this island, they are my compatriot, it says you did well to shoot me otherwise I would shock and die seeing the shark's sharp teeth". Then she laughed loudly, but when she saw our serious face she stopped it. She threw the bird on the Braque and came to take Jim's paddle as he was tired. Paddling she asked me "do you know the sharks? I think there are many kinds of sharks in the seas and oceans of the world, it is a very dangerous and powerful animal, and I don't think anybody can fight with it". I knew all the replies to her questions, but I had focused on shark hunting, I was so stressful that I did not reply to her. She talked all the time no matter that there was nobody to listen to her except herself.

It was noon when we arrived at the rocks, we threw pieces of the hunted bird into the water and waited for the sharks. Angela was frustrated due to our silence so I told her "On the way coming here you asked me some questions about the sharks".

-"So?", she said.

- " I want to tell you", I said.

She was very curious and said "well, I am listening to you".

-"First of all, sharks origin dates back to more than two billion years; second, more than four hundred seventy kinds of sharks live in the seas and ocean, and if you can fist a shark on its snout it will lose its balance and will escape; of course if you have the time", I said

-"On the Braque, if I see the sharks I should test this last point", she said and laughed.

Two hours passed, but there was nothing.

- "Is there any shark around here?" Jim asked.

- "Going to see Hakan and Ramiz I had seen some of them. I hope they have smelled the blood and come around", I said.

We waited for a long time, but it was disappointing. Angela was angry and believed that we should do something as it was possible the sea get stormy. So we decided to come back to the camp and postpone shark hunting for another day. My friends were tired of waiting, but I did not like to put away my goals and come back, I wanted to stay there and wait for the sharks but I feared they lose their way without me. We collected our stuff and came down the rock, we passed a few steps when Angela said "I have left one of the water bottles, you should go, and I will join you". She went over the rocks while suddenly she shouted "the sharks, the sharks". Soon we joined her and saw four big sharks were coming toward us. When they reached the bottom of the rocks they started to search the corpse of the dead bird. They were around us and we should do something immediately because if they could not find any meat they would come back soon. We selected one of them and shot in its head, we had hunted it with the first shooting and Jim screamed happily. We selected the second one and shot it, but it was smart and was swimming quickly but we killed it finally. While shooting I looked at Jim and Angela, they were very angry with the sharks and were seriously shooting. Angela had gotten crazy and was crying and cussing while she was shooting. After killing the second shark I said "that is enough, the others have escaped" but Angela was still crying and shooting the dead sharks. I took her gun by force and said "don't waste the bullets, they are dead". She sat down on a stone and cleaning her tears, she said "how I can control myself while these sharks ripped the poor injured passengers of the crashed plane in front of my eyes". I took her hand and said "they are innocent. Let's go to bring the Braque".

Angela and I should go to bring the Braque while Jim should stay there to shoot if a shark came back. Fortunately, nothing happened and tying the rope to the sharks' tails I swam to the Braque and we started to paddle. Jim should go back to the camp through the island way to be sure Demet is okay and to make a fire if it got dark and we were late. Paddling was difficult as the Braque was pulling the sharks and we were moving slowly. I was worried that the other sharks attack us, smelling the killed ones we were carrying, but everything was okay and after a hard time we arrived in the camp at midnight with the help of a fire Jim and Demet had made on the coast.

The next day early in the morning we were ready to cut the sharks into pieces and get their fat. The samurai sword was sharp enough to cut the sharks as easily as cutting a piece of cheese. We separated their meat and fat, then pour them into the clay dishes Angela had made before and put them on the fire. We melted all the fat and poured them into the frames we had made of bamboos, for the wick of the candles we used the strings Angela had made of the goat wool. After three hours the fats were hard and Jim opened one of the frames. Separating the bamboos we had the candles. We lit the candles with the lighter. They were not like the candles I had already seen, they were smelling bad, but they were light as a real candle. Jim suggested to be silent like the Americans for one minute to respect Edison who had invented electricity. For me we should be silent to respect the soul of the person who had made candles for the first time not Edison.

That night we had the dinner under the bower where Angela and Demet had cooked fish soup and seashell for the first time. The candles had made light everywhere. The sound of clay dishes and wooden spoon were pleasant. The girls had made a great meal and a colorful table full of different fruits because of the new invention we had. During the dinner, Angela said "to make the room light, I am going to make a fat-burning light, then we will have no problem of pouring the wax and burned candles". Everybody was happy to hear that.

After the supper and before anybody else wanted to talk about a topic I stood up and said " every day all of us together and hand in hand can invent and make new things, but have you ever thought how long we could continue? Are you going to stay here for the rest of your life? Did you forget your families? Our main work is to make something to leave here. Why don't you accept that we belong to somewhere else. It is time to do something to leave here. Be sure still there are some who have not believed our death. I am going to start making a ship from tomorrow and be sure if you leave me alone I will do it myself". Then I said "do you want to help me?"

Jim stood up, I was happy about this, but he put his hand on his waist and said "Yashar, there is no doubt that you are very intelligent, also we are sure that you were the man who saved all of us and we owe this comfortable life to you, but I am too old that you think, I cannot accept the risk of passing the ocean or facing the sharks or sea storms". His eyes got into tears and continued "I am sure my relatives supposed me as a dead one, so it is not important any more that where I will be buried. I want to live in comfort in my last days of life". He sat down and I looked at Demet, she started to describe the status we had that without me they could never make it. She made me disappointed. Angela wanted to say something, but I left the camp without listening to her. I was feeling very bad, I did not know may be they were right and I was very unfair to compare them with myself, I expected them to be like me. That night and for the first time I wished to be alone on that island and nobody could understand my feelings. I sat down on the wharf and was thinking of my loneliness when Angela came and sat beside me quietly. She wanted to take my hand, but I passed it away. She put her hand on my shoulder and said "I wish you had enjoyed the pleasure of breathing, then you could understand me that what a delightful feeling one has who lives with you. I know you think a lot about your family and this bothers you, but have you ever thought that if you cannot pass the ocean you will never can think about them? You are alive here and live, but if you die...why you don't want to accept this, they all think you as a dead one, they don't think about you anymore".

Although I knew she was right, I got annoyed and said "I am alive, I breathe and my wife should know this, everybody should know that I am alive, and there are many people dying for their valuable aims, I never fear of death". She saw that I was serious so she put her head on my shoulder and started crying. I couldn't stand her crying, I cleaned her tears. She sighed and said "do you want to leave me alone on an island where you made a comfortable life for me. I wished you knew what a pretty world I have made with you", then she stood up and she shook her head and continued "I know I will never be with you". Then she went to the camp. That night was one of my worst one in my life, I felt myself very helpless. I couldn't think so I sat down on the wharf and closed my eyes. I could hear the sea waves, they helped me to feel calm. I sat down there until I went to sleep.

I dreamed my wife. She had stood in front of me wearing a white dress and looking at me angrily. I told her " Negar! My darling, I am alive, believe me I am alive and I want to come back home but I cannot". She opened her arms to me and with a begging voice she said "I am sure you are alive, come back home as soon as possible. Come to be with your son". Then she disappeared. I got up suddenly. This was the first time I had dreamed her after the plane crash. I got that I had cried in the dream. I was sure she was waiting for me and I got more hope to come back home.

Build the first boat

In the morning when I got up I sat down the wharf and thought about my last night decision. I was annoyed of the others carelessness. I wanted to make a big strong Braque and start the travel. Far distance from my family was bothering me, especially as I had dreamed my wife and I was sure that she was waiting for me. I returned to the camp, my friends were eating the breakfast. Seeing me Angela stood up and went to her room with a frown. I sat beside Jim and drank a glass of milk. He put his hand on my shoulder and said "I know what you feel, but believe me we should stay here, we shouldn't leave here, think about it. Be sure God loves all his creatures and thinks about them. I am sure they will come to take us, wait for that".

I smiled and he thought that I agreed with him, but I could not wait for others help. After the breakfast, I took the sword and a gun and said I would go to see my friends for two weeks to help them make a Braque and a house. Of course I did not have such an idea just I wanted to go to the south part of the island to make the Braque by myself without telling them anything. So I took my personal stuffs and other needed tools, I started my way to the bamboo forest.

I needed higher bamboos to make a big new Braque so I cut them into big pieces. The bamboo forest was in the south part of the island and very close to the coast, so I had no problem to carry them. I was very motivated so I never felt tired. Up to the afternoon I had collected many bamboos on the coast and I had made a shelter too for night sleep. To hide the fire smoke, I had to eat just fruits during the day, but there was no problem to make a fire and cook something for dinner. That night I was alone in my shelter and thought about my friends, and what they were doing. I knew Demet was talking about the goats and the problems of their feeding. Most probably Jim was talking about making big jars to make wine. I had suspected his works during the last two weeks and I was sure he wanted to make wine. But I was sure Angela was very depressed and missed me. She loved me in an unbelievable way. That night I slept with lots of thoughts and dreams.

The next morning I got up energetically and started to make the Braque. Making the camp, I had encountered with an interesting phenomenon accidently and that was bending of bamboos beside the fire. I was going to use this technique to bend the head and tail of the bamboos for the floor and the body of the Braque. To do so, I cut the bamboos along the Braque and then put the other ones transversely. Of course bending the bamboos was not an easy job. I had to heat and tie them to bend up to sixty degree. I cut them in dimensions I needed before bending and I had selected the dimension in such a way that I could make a rectangular sharp head Braque. I was going to put some sharp head trunks under the Braque to keep it over the sea level and increase its weight to stand against the storms and winds. The tree trunks were as the chassis to add them the sail rig in their hole. I could even make a little shelter against the hot sun and raining. The most difficult part of making the Braque was cutting the trees in the forest and carrying them to the coast as I do not have enough energy and the proper tools.

Due to hot and humid weather it was very difficult to work, but I had decided to leave the island and this had motivated me to keep on the work. With simple tools I made the floor of the Braque within a month that would be done in a week if my friends had helped me. I postponed the rest of the work to carry the tree trunks. Ending the Braque I stood beside it and watched it over, it was marvelous. I sat down on the

Braque and thought about my friends. I had been far away from the camp more than what I had promised and I was annoyed why they had not been worried for me, they had not come to see me. I was annoyed by Angela more than the others as she used to express her loved feelings. I thought I should forget them for their unfaithfulness, I had decided to leave the island as soon as I could finish making the Braque to leave them alone to do whatever they want to.

That day the weather was cloudy in the afternoon, so I tied the Braque to a tree to keep it safe against the wind and storm. I wanted to come back to my shelter when I felt Angela was calling me, but I did not see anybody. I thought I had an illusion and I heard a sound due to the wind, but I heard the same voice again and when I returned I saw Angela running towards me from the forest. She hugged me and began to cry like a baby who had not seen her mother for a long time, she was kissing me. Then it started to rain, but we were still hugging and kissing, this was the first time I could not stop kissing her.

That night it was raining hard and the sky was lightning, but I had sat down beside the fire and regardless of other things looking at Angela's eyes, which were shining while she was grilling the birds we had already hunted.

- "You came to see me too late, I did not think that you were so apathetic", I told her.

She smiled and said "it was the first week I knew that you were not with your friends".

- "How did you know this?", I asked.

-"A few days after you left us, Hakan came to the camp again and said Reza was really sick and I should go to visit him. At first I did not believe and I wanted to shoot him, but when I saw his insist I took up the bag and went with him", she said.

When I arrived in the cave I saw that Reza had appendicitis infection and I had to get it out as soon as possible.

- "So?", I said.

- "Well, I saved Reza from death and when I asked about you they said you had not been there and I got it that you were busy in a part of the island", she kept on.

 - "How did you get his appendicitis?", I asked.

"With a shaving blade you had in your bag", she said laughing.

I was astonished and asked " how did you make him numb?".

-"Numb? Your friends took his hands and legs and I cut his side and took out the appendicitis while he was screaming, then I sew it with string and needle I got in your bag. Poor man, he was bloody, your friends got vomiting to see all that blood", she said and laughed.

Angela was telling the story in such a way that I got a bad feeling and vomiting, but she laughed and said "hey man! I am kidding, how can one do surgery without numbing? Reza got numb eating an extract of a fruit of Indonesia islands and I did my job without any problem", she laughed again.

Eating the food Angela left the shelter for a while to go to a toilet, coming back she was completely wet and was breathing hard. It was strange, at first I suspected her, but then I thought may be running in the rainy weather made her wet and tired. So I did not ask her anything. I had been far from her for a long time, so I hugged her pleasantly and while I did not want the time to pass I slept beside the fire.

I got up in the morning, it was not raining anymore and there was no storm. I looked at Angela, she had slept in my hug like a baby. I wanted to stand up when she opened her eyes and said good morning to me with a smile. "Did you sleep well last night?", I asked.

-"Your arms are the calmest and safest place in the world I have ever seen, I can take a rest well beside you", she said.

-"Last night you have told many of these stories, you did not let me sleep, that's enough, now we should have something for eating", I said.

Angela stood up and went out of the shelter, but she came back in a hurry and said "Yashar! The storm has taken the Braque!".

I left the shelter quickly, the storm had torn the Braque rope and had taken it far away into the sea that I could not see anything. That was a shocking view, I could not stand it, and I lost my control and sat down. I did not know what to do, it was too hard for me to cope with it, I had worked hard for one month and now I had lost everything. I was so angry that I was fisting the sands. Angela sat down beside me and cutting a coconut with the knife I had given her, she said "It normally happens, don't worry, be sure it was good for you, I don't know maybe God wanted to warn you to stay on the island for a while...". While she was busy cutting the fruit, she was advising me with a special feeling of relaxing. Her carelessness was strange for me and in a moment I got an idea. I stood up and looked at the other end of the rope I had tied to the tree. I was right, it had been cut by a knife. The rope was too strong to be torn by wind or storm. I got the head of the rope in my hand and looked at Angela with irritation. She was talking without stop, then she looked at me with astonishment when she got tired. She had guessed of my suspect so she got embarrassed and said with a smile "this rope was not as strong as the old ropes". She smiled again.

-"Why did you leave the shelter last night?", I asked.

She paused and said "well, I had to".

-"Why?", I asked.

-"For the toilet", she said with a fake laugh.

-"But you never do so in a rainy weather", I said.

She was silent for a while and I continued "am I really an idiot?", before she could say anything I shouted "you crazy, I had worked for one month to make the Braque, what I should do with your works, I lost all my hope".

-"When I did not see you with your friends, I knew that you were busy making the Braque. I cried a lot for a few days and looked for you then I found you. Then after every day I came here to was watch you from far distance. It was pleasant for me. Do you know what it means? I can't stand to be far from you, why don't you want to know this?", then she started to cry, but I got my stuff and left her without saying anything.

Angela had disobliged me, cutting the rope she had cut my relations from the rest of the world so that I was careless of the others and did not even think of leaving the island. During the days I was walking purposeless in the forest and at nights I was sleeping beside the fire without thinking about anything. I hated everybody and thought that they had not appreciated all I had done for them. I lived in the forest like "Robinson Cruise" for two months so that I was like him. Sometimes I wanted to go to the old crashed airplane, but I saw Angela, waiting for me, had sat down beside the fire. I was hatred of her and her love, I preferred to be alone, but I was controlling her from far distance. Demet and Hakan were meeting each other secretly and had a good relationship. Once I got so close to them secretly that I could hear their breath. In the shrubbery behind the camp, Jim had made a wine storage for himself in the vats Angela had made. He would like to spend a few hours there every day. Of course Ramiz and his friends were stealing his products, but Angela had lost his happy mood, she forgot to laugh as before, most of the time she was alone and worried. She was looking around all the time, seemed she was waiting for me. She was coming to the forest and praying, she was talking about me and her love, she was singing songs to adore me and sometimes she was crying but I could not forget her work. One day I was passing by the crashed plane when I saw her that had made a fire and was talking to somebody. I was curious, so I went closer. I watched her carefully and saw that she was talking to me. At first I was laughing since she was talking in a way as if I was with her and talking to her. But as I listened more I knew that she had gotten crazy. She was passing her happy days with her fantasy love until the afternoon and while she was saying goodbye, she said "my darling, forgive me if the lunch was not delicious, I know but I promise to make a delicious food for the next time. If you let me, I want to leave now as maybe the others are worried". Then she kissed her fantasy love and left there. After she went I cried for a long time because I was sure that she had lost her wisdom due to my love. She knew that I liked the odd days of the week, so she was coming beside the crashed plane and was passing the whole of the day with her fantasy love. At first I was careless of this event, but then I got used to go there on odd days, waiting for her behind the trees and if she could not come I was getting crazy. She was coming and talking to me, but I was just crying, sometimes I wanted to attach and hug her, a few times I decided but I could not and just cried. One night I was so depressed that I decided to go to the camp at midnight. I went into Angela's room, I closed the door quietly, but suddenly she said "hi my darling, you are here to sleep with me, come on, I have always waited for you". I was astonished, but then I knew that she was talking to her fantasy love. That night I cried a lot in the dark room until Angela got sleep. I came closer to her, her tears were shining in the moonlight. I kissed her and to show my presence I cut my long tresses hair and put it over her head. That night I forgave her and prayed for her. I was not hatred for her anymore.

Old woman carcass

I left her and out of the camp, I sat down by the wall. I felt Angela's depression was my fault, so I cried a lot and got sleep there. I dreamed an old Asian woman with white hair and a pearl necklace. She came to me and sat down in front of me, bowing three or four times she said "Young man! It is many years I have been waiting for you, I need your help. Please give me a hand!".

-"Who are you? What can I do for you?" I asked her.

She stood up and going far away, she said "you can find me in the northeast of the island. A big gift will be for you".

She said this and disappeared. I got up at once. I was breathing hard and I had sweated. Up to that time I had dreamed a lot, but none of them was as clear as this one. Her tone of voice was in a way that I could not stand against her request. Also the "gift" was interesting for me and I wanted to start the adventurous story. The sun was rising so before anybody could see me, I left there.

The camp was near to the site the old woman had talked about and I could arrive in there soon. On my way to that area I heard her voice several times. I was thinking who she was and what I could do for her. Surely she was not one of the passengers of the plane and could be alive for such a long time. After one hour I arrived in the northeast of the island. It was a wide area full of trees, so densely grown beside each other that looked like a natural castle and had made difficult to pass the way. I had to cut the trees and bushes with the sword to find a way to pass through. It was two hours I was busy cutting the trees and searching a thing that I was not sure of it, the only thing I knew was that there would be something, a sign of that old woman. I put my stuff on the ground and stared at the tall trees standing with honor in front of me. Carefully looking I got it that they were all fruit trees that I had not ever seen. I did not know how they had been planted there and grown so densely beside each other. The other strange thing was the parallel line of the trees like the apple gardens in my homeland, so I was sure that somebody had planted them. I was curious and ate one of the fruits. It was sweet. I was serious again and I decided to find out the secret of that old woman even if I would have to stay on the island for the rest of my life.

That day I searched the area until the afternoon, but I could not find out anything to be a sign of that old lady. I was too tired to eat something so I got sleep soon. I dreamed the old woman again. She came closer and said "my son, you are very close to me. Don't be hopeless. Try it!".

- "I just want to leave here. Could you help me?", I said.

- "You will leave here with an incredible health", she said with a smile.

I got up in the morning, I got the dream in a good omen. So I started the search again and I cut the bushes and trees to widen the way to go through when all of a sudden a wide area was in front of me with a ruined cottage in the middle. I pulled the breech block of the gun and quietly came closer to the cottage. It was clear it had been ruined a long time ago and nobody lived there. I opened the damaged door of the cottage with the head of the gun and entered the cottage. A part of the ceiling had been ruined, everywhere was full of cobwebs. A wooden box was seen in one corner. In the old box I could see an old women cloth and some colorful clothes. Some of them had been damaged through the time. I opened the other boxes too, but there was not a useful thing inside. Among the old clothes I could find out a notebook written in oriental handwriting. I preferred to show the notebook to Angela, I thought we could find out the old lady's secret if we could read it. I turned the pages over when I noticed some pages had been torn, I got them in the first wooden box in a white cloth. I got them, put them in my pocket and left the cottage to search the area around. There was storage behind the cottage, a damaged door locked with a lock and chain. I knew I could open it with a little kick but I shot the gun. There were lots of stuff for carpentry, a big saw for cutting the trees, an ax, a hand drill, a chipper, a peg and a hammer. I was happy and I was sure this time I could make a ship to pass through the ocean as I had promised Angela.

The old woman had fulfilled her promise. I was very hopeful to find the treasure. I did not think the stuff I had found was the treasure she had promised me in my dream. So. I left the store and continued my search to find the treasure. Behind the cottage I faced with a strange scene. I saw a corpse of an old woman, seemed had died a long time ago, she had died while sitting towards the sea. She had worn a beautiful pearl necklace looked like the one I had seen in my dream. I took the necklace and looked at it carefully. The pearls size and holes had been made skillfully and I could not believe it had been made by a local of that far distant island, but I was sure she was the old woman I had already dreamed who wanted me to help her. I thought what I could do for an old corpse. I looked at her carefully to know the way she had sat and her bones. Putting her hands on her laps she had sat facing to northern rocks of the island, I could not understand anything more. I left the corpse and entered the cottage, I searched inside it carefully, I took out even the wooden floor but there was no treasure.

After a long time of searching the treasure I was very tired and hungry. I sat beside the old woman's corpse and I shouted at her "did you make ridiculous me? Which treasure? Do call these old carpentry tools as treasure?". I stood up and brought some woods and put them in front of the corpse. I cleaned my forehead sweat with my hand and said "you did not fulfill your promise but I know what I should do with you. I want to burn you with all these papers, so you will never be in others' dream to make them ridiculous". Then I took the necklace, I put the woods around the corpse, I took the papers and fired them. There was a mild wind and the lighter got off. I tried several times, but every time I failed. I thought a little, maybe there was wisdom, then I remembered burning corpse is not good in our beliefs so I put the papers and the lighter in my pocket, I threw the woods apart and dug a hole to bury the corpse. I took a piece of the white cloth from the wooden box inside the cottage and wrapped the bones inside it. I buried the corpse and blessed for her soul. I wished she was the last corpse I buried on the island. Then I took up my stuff and started my way to the camp. It was sunset when I arrived in the camp. Angela had sat down beside the gate of the camp and was combing her hair. She saw me from far distance, but she could not know me due to my long hair and beard. When I went closer she called the others and said "my dear Yashar, hey guys, Yashar came back", she ran towards me and kissed me.

Treasure map

When I entered the camp I took a shower and did shaving. That night we had a good meal, Jim brought his best wines for the dinner. We were all together until midnight, Jim and Demet were talking about all the adventures they had all these days. All the time Angela had taken my hand and was just staring at me. Late at night she stood up and said "I know you are very tired and you should take a rest", then she took my hand, we went to her room. When I entered her room, I was surprised. She had written my name in different languages and in big and small letters on many bamboo pieces and had hung from the ceiling. I got more surprised when I saw she had cut the bamboos in a flat form in a way that I did not know how. I looked at her. She smiled and said "I am crazy about you, I wish you knew what feeling a crazy person may have". I looked at her pretty eyes and I felt I was crazy about her too. Without saying anything about the old woman's corpse and her cottage I hugged her and began to kiss her body. That night I got the world joy in her arms and sleeping with her refreshed me.

Once I got sleep, I dreamed the old woman again, she was very glad and thanked me to bury her.

-" You deserve to find out the treasure", she said. Leaving me she added, " you are very close to the treasure, be careful, the papers, the papers, the papers..." then she disappeared.

Tomorrow morning I got up earlier than Angela. She had slept calmly in my arms, with her pretty smile I knew that she had the best dream of her life. A little then she got up and smiled. Up to that day I had never looked at her eyes, she had the most beautiful eyes in the world. I felt spring blossoms and jasmine smell while she got up. I had stared at her in such a way that she laughed and said "hey man! What's up? Good morning!".

I kissed her and said "my dear, I love you so much, when I left you I knew what a precious creature you are. I wish I could bring you all the world jewelry to forgive me. I was unfair. Please forgive me and promise to be always with me, I will love you forever".

She did not expect to hear these exciting words so she stood up and sat beside the bed. Feeling completely confused, she asked "what? Repeat it! Are you sure it is not the effect of last night wine?".

I smiled and said "I did not drink wine last night, you heard it, and I can't describe all your beauties, and you are an angel!". I kissed her forehead and while she was completely confused, I took her hand and we left the room.

Demet was milking the goats and Jim was feeding them with grass. That day and for the first time I had cheese and hot milk for the breakfast. Then I took the lances to go fishing with Angela. Leaving the camp, she took my hand and said "There are lots of things to tell you", then we moved towards the wharf. On the way she said "have you ever asked yourself why I was so happy when you gave me your knife?".

-"I thought that was a custom in your country", I said.

Shaking her head, she said "No! It has a story. When I was a little girl, my grand mom told me about the happenings of the time when she got married. She said one day my grandfather had gone to the city, but coming back to the village, he had forgotten to bring a souvenir for my grandmother, so he gave his knife to her as a fine. I liked this story and though I was a little girl I promised myself to get married to the first person who would give me a gift knife. That day I got the most important dream I had and from that day I fell in love with you". I shook my head and said "Oh! So you were crazy since childhood". I shook my head and laughed. Hitting me with a piece of bamboo she had in her hand, she said "do you laugh at me? Stop there, I will tell you?" and we ran towards the wharf.

We were busy fishing for two hours, of course it was playing and kidding rather than fishing. Angela was looking at me all the day. After catching some fish Angela sat beside the wharf, putting her feet into the water, she blanks me and called me to sit beside her. When I sat down, she kissed me calmly and said "my life Sun! Where were you all these days?". I told all of the adventures I had all the last days. When she knew I wanted to join her, she cried a lot. I cleaned her tears with my hand and tied the old woman's necklace around her neck, then I told all the story of the old woman and finding out her cottage. I remembered the old notebook I had found there. I took it out of my pocket and asked her to read it. It was an old notebook and it was difficult to read some lines, but Angela read it for me. It was the biography of the old woman.

While she was reading the story for me, I could imagine the old woman's face and her corpse. The notebook story dated back to the Second World War, when invading forces of Japan occupied all the islands in Indonesia. Their attack destroyed everything in those islands and many innocent people lost their lives or homeland. The story began this way: "my name is Fatima. I am writing these sentences while I am very sick and I know that I will die very soon. I don't know if anyone accesses this notebook. But I hope who finds out it is a competent one to use. I am sure in a few days I will attach my husband who died many years ago. I dream him every night". At that moment Angela stopped reading and cried. She looked at me and said "poor old woman! I feel how hard years she had passed in loneliness". Of course I thought she was crying as she had imagined herself as the old woman and me as her poor husband. I laughed at her and cleaning her tears we came back to the camp.

After lunch Demet wanted to talk about an issue, but I was so eager of the old woman's story that I excused her and said that I was tired. I went to my room with Angela and she read me the rest of the story: ' when the Japanese forces attacked our village, most of the women jumped into the sea as they feared of being raped by the soldiers. I and my husband "Faroogh" put our stuff into a ship and escaped from the village before the soldiers could arrive in our village. My husband was a farmer and did not know anything about sailing, although we had little chance of life, we thought sinking in the sea was better than being captivated by the enemy. We had accepted our fate, whatever it would be like to be and we did not know what would happen for us. At the end and after one month of sailing in a stormy sea we arrived in this island. We lived here for one year in comfort. During this time our son "Saleh" was born, brought joy and happiness to our life. Unfortunately, this happiness did not last too much and the enemy found us on the island. At first some warships came around the island. They turned around the island for a while and then left here. Those days we hid like rabbits in the some parts of the island. Four months later some planes had war with each other, two of them crashed near the island but nobody could save his life out of the crash. One of the planes was the biggest of all and it seemed the other planes were supporting it. One month later a submarine came to the island, it found something from the crashed plane and they carried it to the island by boats".

Suddenly Angela closed the notebook and looked at me with a surprise.

- "What do you think about?", I asked.

-" Look, the old woman had said you would leave the island with a big wealth. Maybe that wealth is the things they had taken out of the crashed plane. A box full of gold, brilliant diamonds, old coins…..", she said.

-"I don't know, maybe it is, but…..", laughing I said.

- "But what?", she asked.

- "Honestly, I don't think that there is such a treasure. Those things that you say are seen in old stories like myths", I said.

- "So what do you think about it?", she asked.

-"I don't know, but I think they are war ammunitions", I replied.

- "Gee! And if there is such a treasure? What will you do then?", raising up her eyebrows she said.

- "Then I will be very happy!, I said laughing.

- "And then?", she asked.

-"I don't know what a big treasure is waiting for us, but whatever I find, I will share with you!", touching her beautiful hair, I said.

She was happy of my words and opened the notebook to read the rest of the story: "a few days after the submarine left the island, Faroogh went to the shelter where they had hidden the treasure while I was against of it. It took such a long time he came back that I was hopeless. When he came back it seemed he had seen ghosts. He said he had found boxes of gold and jewels. He had brought a pearl necklace for me as he knew I loved to have one. He had wanted me to believe him".

Angela closed the notebook again and while her almond shaped eyes were round, she looked at the pearl necklace she had on her neck.

- "Oh my God! Did you see? Boxes full of gold and jewels, this necklace are one of those treasures", she said.

Then she took me with her hands and kissed me and said some words in her mother tongue that I could not understand. Meanwhile Demet knocked on the door and wanted to enter. Angela hid the notebook under the bed immediately. She entered the room with three beverages and looked with a sly at us and said "I see you both beloved have joined again after some months, may I come in?". Touching her hair, Angela said without any embarrassment "Oh my dear! Come in, better to see you, we were talking about picking the goats' wool, spinning, and weaving blankets and cloth. You are very experienced in these works and I am sure you can be very helpful. We should not sleep on the ground and have a straw mat". Demet was so pleasure of her suggestion that she put the glasses in front of us and started to talk about these issues. We nodded our heads to support her words and this made her to go on talking, but she did not know we were just thinking about the treasure.

That night and after the supper, there was pleasure in the camp. Demet and Jim had wasted their time during the last months and now with Angela's suggestions they were very excited to start a new work. They were talking about the usefulness of goat's milk and wools with excitement. That night Angela got the wine jar in her hand and was filling our glasses. But I got it that she filled Jim and Demet's glasses, but just a little in her glass and mine. I knew that she wanted them to sleep deeply so that we could read the notebook with ease maybe we could find out the treasure that the old woman had promised me.

Jim was so drunk that he had composed some poems about the goats, as if the goats were "the beauty goddess" of the ancient Greek. That night was the most interesting one of my life as we had to pretend to be drunk, to give much more wine to Jim and Demet. Soon Angela's plan got success and they slept deeply. We took them to their bedrooms and drank a glass of wine together for the soul of the old woman. Then Angela started reading the rest of the notebook as follows: "soon after finding out the treasure, Faroogh was not calm and every day he went to the place it was hidden to take out some of it. I was not interested in this event because I could see that how he had changed his behavior, he was not the same man I knew, he never wanted to work to make a happy life for his wife and child. I did not believe in the wealth he had found out as I had a treasure more valuable than any other things in the world and it was my little family and the calm life I already had on that island. My husband had been lazy, he was drinking wine from morning to night, he was busy with his treasure and jewels, while I and Saleh were working on the farm and fishing. He wanted to come back to his homeland and make a better life for me and my son with that treasure; but his happiness lasted just for a short time when the damn planes came back to the island".

At that moment I put my hand on the notebook.

-"What is up?", Angela asked with a surprise.

- "Did you think about the old woman's words? I think I understood some things of her words", I said.

-"What?", she asked.

- "She has written 'he was going to the jewelry hidden place to take some of them out'", I replied.

- "So what?", she asked.

"Well! The treasure is either under water or inside a cave, isn't it?", I said.

- "You are right! What else did you get?", she said with a pause.

- "Another line she has written that 'I did not believe in that treasure my husband was talking about'. Did you think about this sentence?", I asked.

- "No! I care just the translation and I did not get it. So what does it mean?", she asked.

-"It is clear, it means the old woman herself had not seen the treasure and had just heard of the story from her husband", I replied.

- "So what do we conclude then?", she asked with much more surprise.

- "The treasure is where the old woman could not go there and as there is no cave on the island, the treasure is somewhere around the island and underwater", I said with a smile.

She paused for a while and thought. Reviewing the old woman's words in her mind, she smiled and said "you are right man! Surely it is underwater", she said.

- " Oh! So you got it. Go on reading", I said with a squib.

The story went on as follows: "one day there was a big battle between a few war planes and two of them crashed down into the sea and another one fell down in the jungle. Faroogh thought this time he could find out treasure inside the plane again, so he did not listen to me and went to the plane quickly but he could not get what he expected. The pilots had been killed and the planes were full of military ammunition. Faroogh had found an injured soldier among the broken pieces of the Japanese airplane. He had brought him to our cottage to cure his wounds. I was against to take care of that soldier in the house as he was an enemy of my country. But Faroogh said he did this just for the sake of God. We fed him and cured his injuries, he took rest on the bed to be better than before. A few days later we left home and when we came back we found out that the Japanese soldier had got up and had made a mess the whole of the house. He had got the box of treasure Faroogh had hidden. He had sat down beside the dining table and while he was drinking wine he showed us the jewels on the table. Faroogh was angry with his work and wanted to attack him, but he took out his gun and threatened Faroogh. We could not understand his language, but we got what he meant. He wanted much more gold. And when he saw we did not care his request, he pointed his gun toward Saleh. He was very irritated and wanted to kill my innocent son. I was crying and begged Faroogh to listen to him, but he did not intend to show the hidden jewels to the soldier. Being out of patience, the soldier pulled Saleh towards himself and put the gun on his head. Faroogh did not stand it anymore. He asked the soldier to release Saleh, then he would show the place he had hidden the jewels. Then both of them went out. Leaving the cottage Faroogh looked at me and said 'Thanks for everything! Take care of our son'. That moment I did not know why he said so, but later I got he knew he would never come back. He went and I was alone for many years. I wished he would never find the treasure and we had a calm life".

Angela closed the notebook and hugged me while she was crying. The poor old woman had a miserable life story and I was affected too.

Tomorrow morning we got up due to our friends' voice.

- "I did not think the wine was so useless and they got up soon. Maybe they are keen on picking the goat wool. How are they going to do so?", Angela said, rubbing her eyes.

- "I don't know! This is your suggestion, so find a way for them", I said.

- "We should give them your knife and sword, they will be busy for a few days", she said, thinking for a while.

- " Is it possible to pick the wools with a knife?", I asked with a surprise.

- "These crazy guys want a hobby so they can so even if you give a nail clipper to them!", she said while laughing.

Having breakfast Angela recommended all necessaries to Demet and Jim and told them we should go to the forest to find out some plants for coloring the picked wools. Of course she meant to find a cozy place to read the rest of the story. Demet's naughty looks revealed that she had not believed any of Angela's words.

Leaving the camp I took Angela's hand and we went to the wharf. Along the way she was just talking about the problems Demat and Jim may have during picking the goat wool and she was laughing.

- "Poor goats! I am sure I will have to cure all of them coming back in the afternoon". She was laughing all the time she was with me and wanted me to laugh too. It was nine when we arrived at the wharf. There was a mild breeze at the beach. Angela hugged me, she looked at my eyes for a while and said "you don't know how I am happy to be with you. I wish we could be together forever". Then she kissed me. We sat on the wharf and she read the rest of the story of the old woman. It continued as follows: " Faroogh died and left me alone with a kid. I could not even find his corpse to bury. God knows what difficulties I had to treat and grow up our son. But he went as well and left me alone. We had a clam life until he was fourteen. During all these years we witnessed the presence of the pirates on the island, but they were usually walking around the island to fulfill their storage with meat and fruits or to take the reminders of the sank ships to sell as slaves. We witnessed the tsunami twice too, but it was harmless as we lived far away from the beach. I was alone when Saleh was fourteen years old, when he insisted on coming back to our homeland to get married with one of the girls of our tribe. But I was waiting for my husband, though I was sure he would never come back. I did not know even where his bones were but I could not leave him alone on the island. I always wished to be buried beside my husband, but what a pity! I tried to persuade Saleh to forget the travel, but he did not see my tears and started his way in the sea. After a few days I found his boat pieces by the beach with a sign of shark teeth on and I knew that I had lost everything. I believe in God's endless kindness, but I did not know why he bothered me in such a way. It was last year when the pirates came to the island for the last time. My legs were painful, so I could not turn off the fire in time and they had got the smoke and found me finally. When they saw me they got astonished how a woman could live for all these years alone on the island. They had come to get a slave, but when they found I am too old to be a slave they got disappointed. Though they took my goats. I begged them to leave two of them for me to use their milk, but they did not care my cries and took all the animals I had. The next morning, one of them who were a kind man brought two pairs of the goats for me secretly. He was around forty years, and despite my weak eyes, I could see a snake shape scar on his face and a cut on his left ear. I never forget his kindness as my only food was milk. He repaired the roof of the cottage too. Looking at him I felt that my son Saleh had come back. I asked him to leave the pirates and live with me, but he said he was their head and could not do so. Leaving me he put his head on my knees and cried for a while. Touching his head, I saw a mole on his neck, the one like what my son, Saleh, had. I noticed that he was my son who had come to see me after all these years. At first he denied the truth, but when I swore him to be honest, he kneeled in front of me, cried and asked me to forgive him for all these years he had left me alone with all the difficulties I had. He did not know I was not annoyed by him and I had always wanted a successful and happy life for him. That afternoon Saleh told me how he had been caught by the pirates on his way and had been forced to work for them for many years. He told me the pirates lost their head who was a cruel man and they had selected Saleh as a head of the group to attack the alien ships and to loot their goods. He had married with a girl of our tribe and they had a son. His name was Faroogh to keep his father's name memorable. Saleh told me he had been tired of this work and after his last trip he was going to take me with him to make me a happy life. I insisted to take me with him as I was eager to see my grandson as soon as possible. But he said he did not want his friends know anything about the story and he would come back to take me. It was night when he left me alone again with tearing eyes. Now that I am writing these sentences it is a long time when my son has left me; every day I sit beside the cottage looking to the gulf to see his ship but there is no news. I wish I never let him leave me alone. Today I feel I will die. I opened the door of the fold to let the goat to go to the forest, to be free. I have no power to write anymore. I will sit beside the cottage; if I die, my corpse will witness coming of my son. I wished there was one to wrap my corpse in a white cloth I have inside the wooden box and bury me, then I would give him a good reward. That cloth was a commemoration of my husband, Faroogh. I no longer……..".

Here, Angela said "what a bad end! So where is the treasure? I think death had not let her to write anything more. Poor old woman! She did not use the treasure and did not help us to find it out!".

- "I am happy she got her last dream", I said.

-"How? Did you do anything for her?", she asked with a smile.

- "She wished to be buried in a white cloth. And I did so while I had no idea of this before", I said.

- "So you got a gift of that corpse, did not you?", she asked laughing.

I nodded my head and gave her the pieces of the paper I had found inside the cloth. Angela took them and read them carefully, then she stood up and while screaming loudly and happily started jumping up and down. I asked the reason and she hugged me and kissed me several times. Then, with eyes full of tears she said "the old woman has gifted you in these papers and they will show us the place of the hidden treasure, even her son did not know there". I got shocked for a moment.

- "Hey man! What is up? Why are not you happy?", she asked when she saw my unusual state.

-"I am happy! But just....", I said.

- "Just what?", she asked.

- "That day I wanted to burn her corpse with these papers. I tried several times but I failed with a breeze and I gave it up. There was a mystery here, wasn't there? Maybe her soul was beside me, wasn't it?", I said.

- "Let it be wherever it wants, the most important thing is that you have got your reward and the treasure belongs to you now".

- "You share this treasure too, I had promised to divide in half whatever I find", I said.

She put the papers in my pocket and sitting beside the wharf she said "what will I do with jewels? I just want you, you are my life and without you none of the treasures of the world are worthy for me".

I sat down beside her and said "Do you mean I am very worthy and I don't know? Maybe I should believe in it" and I laughed.

She looked at me deeply and said "I wish you knew how wonderful feeling I have for you".

I asked how with a gesture.

She sighed deeply and said "you are so good in my mind that I think none of the beauties of the world can be so, you are so great that I see your sprit greater than the galaxies, you are so strong that can make possible every impossible thing, you are so kind that ......".

I put my hand on her mouth and said " Stop it! Don't exaggerate too much. On the contrary, I am very inefficient. This is you to make things seem greater than they are". Then kidding, I said "Maybe it is due to your eyes' strong lens, I think your ancestors were Asian eagles or vultures" and I laughed at her.

It was noon when we returned the camp. Unexpectedly, Demet and Jim had finished picking the goat wool and were busy washing them.

- "I had told you they were crazy, I bet they have injured all the goats", Angela said with a surprise.

-"Bet on what?", I asked.

- "On whatever you say", she said.

I thought a little and said "If you lose, you will sing and dance for us after the dinner, okay?"

- "Okay! But just for you and when we are alone", she said with a smile.

We approached them, Demet said "although we picked all the wool, but there was not too much". Angela looked at the collected wool and said with an ironic voice "these are too little to weave blankets for all, I wish we had so many goats!". Demet looked at Angela meaningfully and said "I think two blankets would be enough, one for me and another one for Jim". Angela did not understand her, so she asked with a surprise, "What about me and Yahsar?". "Lover pigeons do not need any blanket, they always sleep in their hugs and their nest is warm and comfortable". I did not like Demet's tone of voice because I had seen her loves with Hakan in the jungle several times. She did not know the story, if she did, she could not dare to talk to us like that. I decided to give a lesson to her as soon as possible. To change the topic, I asked "how did you pick all these wool without scissors? It would be too difficult, am I right?". She began to tell the whole story with eager, while Angela left us secretly to inspect the goats and when she saw they had done the work in its best way she joined us embarrassed. Her face was really interesting. I gestured her that she had lost the bet. She did not want to accept so she smiled in a fake way and shrugged her shoulders. Jim spread the washed wool on the bamboos, broke his colic and cleaned his forehead sweat and said "to thank this great discovery we should have a great meal and celebrate". I knew that Demet and Jim had worked from early in the morning and they were very tired, so I said "I and Angela will make the dinner ready. Of course we will have wine as well". It was in the afternoon when Angela and I took the guns and we both went to the forest to hunt birds and collect fruits.

Along the way, we talked just about the plan for the next day. We decided to leave the camp secretly the next day and go to the rocky part of the island in the north, where the old woman had written about in her notebook to find out the treasure. We should care Ramiz and his friends too, because we had seen previously they watch us over to find out what we were doing. Nobody should know about the treasure. Since I had decided to find the treasure I was very excited about the scene I may see there; I did not know what I should do.

It was cloudy when we came back to the camp. Jim was making a fire under the bower. Demet was taking the goats to the fold. An hour later we were all around the dinner table. It was raining and we were eating the roasted meat. Demet was telling us about the memories of her travels. Angela was going to fulfill the wine glasses for Demet and Jim as before. We wanted them to drink full and go to a deep sleep so that we could leave the camp before they get up. It was nine when both Jim and Demet were sleepy after drinking a little wine and went to sleep beside the supper table. It was strange because the previous time it took a while they got sleep. I looked at Angela. She raised up and down her eyebrows, then she showed me a white powder she had inside a cloth and said, "I was not in a good mood to fill their wine glasses until the midnight and listen to their ridiculous sayings". Then she looked at the powder and said, "I had made Reza unconscious before his surgery with this powder". I got astonished more and asked "what does it mean? Why did you do this with Jim and Demet? Is it dangerous for them?". She threw the cloth towards me and said" Don't worry! It is safe. They will get up tomorrow after we leave here." "And if they won't?"", I said. Taking Demet on her shoulder, she laughed and said " You know how to bury dead ones!" again, she started laughing and under the rain, she took Demet to her bedroom while she was completely unconscious. I did not like her tone of voice. I put the cloth in my pocket and took Jim to his bedroom. When I entered his room, I remembered Ramiz and his friends. They were always watching us from the west part of the camp, hiding behind the trees. I got an interesting idea. I went to the wine store. I took a wine vat to their shelter. I thought the next day when they would find the wine there, they would be happy and busy of celebration. To prolong their celebration I poured a little of the white powder inside the vat as well.

It was severely raining and when I entered my room, I was completely wet. I took off my cloth; when I wanted to turn off the candles to go to bed, Angela entered my room with a wine glass. She drank a little of the wine and said "You are very interested in seeing an oriental girl dance, aren't you?" Then she began to sing and dance. She was turning around me like a butterfly and was singing the folklore poems with her wonderful voice. I was so excited that took the wine glass and drank all the wine and started dancing. That night we enjoyed a lot and then went to sleep.

I got up the next day with Angela's touching, she had laid down beside me and was touching my hair. I got up and sat down by the bed. "My Lord! Can we find out the hidden treasure today?", I said raising my hands.

Angela looked at me meaningfully and said "What are you going to do after finding the treasure?".

-"I will take my share and will enjoy my life forever", I said with a smile.

- "With whom are you going to enjoy?", she asked.

- "It is clear, with my family", I replied.

- "What will you do if I give my share to you? Do you get married with me?", she asked with a pause.

For a moment I saw her beautiful breasts over the straw mat, I said, "If somebody asks me the craziest person all over the world, be sure I will show you! You are pretty, talented with academic grade, you can get married to a young man from your country, and you can have a comfortable life forever, especially now that you are going to be a wealthy lady. Believe me, you bother yourself more than me".

She stood up and wearing her cloths she said "do you think nobody wanted to marry with me? NO! There were many rich men wanted to marry me who had a private island. Why don't you want to understand that I love you. I was waiting for you for many years and I was dreaming you all the time. Do you remember the first time I saw you on the plane? I was very excited. When you told me hello you did not know how good I was feeling, even the plane crash was not important for me. Do you why? Because I had found you and I wanted to die, but to be in your arms. You know when I came out of the plane, I left my dad and brother to look for you".

Saying some things in her mother tongue and crying, she left the room. I did not know what I should do with that crazy girl. I put on my cloth, taking the necessary stuff I left the room. I checked out Jim and Demet. Our plan was successful and they were sleeping. So we went out of the camp with ease. Along the way Angela did not talk and we continued our way for two hours to arrive at the north part of the island, where big and small rocks were seen in every corner. That day was a chance day for us, the sea was calm, and the waves hitting the beach were not very strong. For one hour we searched all the holes in the rocks, but we could not find any boxes. Angela was out of mood, she sat down on a rock and said "where is this damn treasure?".

-" Do you remember the old woman's writings? I am sure it will be under water!", I said.

- "What do you mean? If it is under water, then the sea algas have covered it", she said with a surprise.

-"What if there is a cave under water?", I said with a smile.

- "You are right! So what should we do now?", she said.

Putting all the stuff I had on a rock, I asked "Can you swim under water?".

She said yes with her head.

-"So save your breath and follow me", I said.

Then we jumped into the water. Under the water, there were coral rocks and colorful fishes. It was really amazing, I felt I was in another world. We did not have diving tools so we had to come up to the water to breathe again. We searched the whole of the place the old woman had said for half an hour bur there was not any sign of the cave. We were very tired, but we were too tempted of the treasure to leave the work and come back to the camp. It was noon and we were too hungry to move. Angela noticed that I was out of mood, so she took some fruits out of her bag and said "British people say a hungry man is an angry one. Let's have some fruits, then we should decide. God is great!". These words made me feel strange and I closed my eyes and asked God to help us to find the treasure. Angela was cutting the fruits and giving me with her usual smile. She was enjoying to give me service. Eating the fruits I saw a big rock like a dolphin, a hundred meters far from us. It was very interesting and looked like a cut stone. Angela got my careful look and eating a piece of fruit she asked "what are you looking at?". Pointing to the rock I said "The rock is very interesting. I like sculpturing since childhood and once I carved a statue with my mom's kitchen knife. She punished me a lot instead of encouraging".

- "Why punishment?", she asked with a surprise.

-"I had broken her knife", laughing I said.

-"What had you made?", she asked.

-"A dolphin's head", I replied.

Suddenly Angela stood up and shouted with joy "A dolphin's head! A dolphin's head". I remembered the old woman's writings that the treasure is under a rock look like a dolphin's head. We jumped into the water in a hurry and arrived at the rock. I was so excited that my heartbeat was faster than before. I thought if this time we failed I would have a heart attack. I looked at Angela, she was excited too and was panting. I kissed her happily and after a deep breath we both jumped into the water. Two meters under the sea level and exactly under the rock there was a tunnel made by stones fell on each other. Angela pointed me to go through the tunnel, but I took her hand to come to the water surface.

- "We have found the cave entrance, why did not you go through?", she asked with a surprise.

- "First, we have nothing for defense, we are not sure about the probable dangers facing us. Second, maybe there are other tunnels inside the cave, we may lose our way and forever, and we can't find the way to come out of the water".

-"You are right, so what should we do right now?", she said after a little thinking.

-"If we had rope we could put it along the way not to lose the way. But we can do something else", I said.

 -"What?", she asked.

-"We enter the tunnel and if there is another way inside it we come back immediately and make another decision. Just be careful not to be tempted to take danger for the treasure', I said.

She accepted and I took my knife. We breathed deeply and went into the water. The tunnel width was about two meters and the way the rocks had connected each other made it clear that it had been made by natural factors. Fortunately, there was no branch inside the tunnel and after swimming about ten meters, the sea was brighter than before and I knew that we were close to the water surface. Going through the tunnel I turned back to see if Angela needed help but she wanted me to go on the way. We swam for a while and reached the water surface. When we came out of the water we saw there was a cave made as the stones had fallen on one another. The height was about three meters, anyway, it was not a safe place. An earthquake could collapse it down. Air and light were available inside the cave. I went closer and I saw we could pass through the hole in there, but since it was facing the rocks and it was high we couldn't go down without a rope. The landslide danger was probable. I was looking at the ceiling and the wall of the cave when Angela called me "Yashar! Come here". In a rather darker corner of the cave there were four metal boxes. I went closer and saw the broken cross sign of the Nazi army in the Second World War. The door of one box was completely open and the jewels inside were amazing. My heart was beating so fast that I felt it would be stopped. Each of the boxes had four locks that had been already broken. Maybe Faroogh had done it. We opened the other boxes. It was unbelievable to see all those priceless jewels in front of us. We pulled the boxes to sunlight. The light reflected from the jewels made inside the cave lighter than before. Suddenly Angela screamed of fear and jumped into the air as she had sat down on two corpses on the corner of the cave. The corpses had been rotted, but from their cloths it was clear that one of them was Faroogh and the other one was the Japanese soldier that had come to take the boxes out of the cave. There was a knife in Faroogh's chest and the soldier's skull had been broken. It was clear that finding the treasure, they had fought and killed each other. It was an interesting scene. On the one hand, there was Angela who was happy with jewels in her hands; and on the other side there were the rotted bodies of two men who had killed each other for the gold. If I had a camera to take a photo of that scene, I was sure it would be a winner in many photo competitions. I was sure if somebody else had found all those jewels, had been tempted to kill Angela to take all the wealth for himself.

The jewels seemed to be very old and antique. Maybe the German submarine had found them from the sank old ships, or perhaps from the ships they had attacked during the war. It was very strange for me that why all those jewels had been hidden there. Did they fear the enemy could find them? Or did they want to take them out after the war? I guessed they had hidden the boxes and then fought with the enemy, when all had been killed and nobody could know the secret of the jewels. Angela was busy with the jewels for a long time and when she got tired she said " Hey man! What are you going to do with all these jewels?".

- "Half of it is yours. Do you have any idea?', I said with a smile.

- "I think we should stay here, then we will be the richest people on the earth", she said with a smile.

- "Don't you think that to live as a rich person is better than to die as a rich man? How can you use these jewels on this far distant island and be a rich person?', I asked.

- "Well! We should take the jewels with ourselves", she thought for a while and said.

-"How can we take them that nobody is aware of?", I asked.

She thought for a while and when she could not find a way she shrugged her shoulders. "I have a good idea! Before it gets dark, we should come back to the camp. Tomorrow we make some ropes by tree barks and then take the boxes out of the cave. Just be careful not to talk anything about this story to anybody or.....", I said.

She interrupted my words and said "Do I look as an idiot one? Am I crazy to talk about it?".

-"I mean we should be very careful", I said.

She was listening to me carefully, so she asked "and then?".

- "Then nothing! We will take our own share and hide it in a place to take it whenever needed. But I think the best thing we can do is to deliver the jewels to the Indonesia government because it is their national wealth", I replied.

She paused for a while and confirmed my idea with her head and said "maybe I will do the same thing but...".

-"But what?", I asked.

She paused for a while and said "I still have my own idea. If you get married me all the treasure will be for you. I won't want anything for myself".

I sighed and said "You crazy girl!". And then I went towards the corpses. I did not want to talk about the issue anymore. She got it and changed the topic and asked "So what should we do with the corpses? Shouldn't we bury them here?".

- "We should make two big baskets to carry them out of the cave. They have been far from their families, so they should be burned beside them", I said.

That night I was so tired that couldn't finish dinner, especially as I was very excited about finding the treasure I had drunk too much wine. I decided to go to bed, due to drinking too much I was drunk and sleepy,

I saw Angela in two bodies in front of me, and then I laughed and asked "which of you is my pretty Angela?". I wanted to put my hand on her shoulder, but feeling dizzy I fell down on her. She had not seen me like that before. She took my arm and took me to my room. She helped me to go to bed and touching my face, she was murmuring amorously words in my ears. I enjoyed that moment a lot as though I was flying in the sky. She laid beside me and hugged me. Her kisses made me feel to be in the top of the sky. She made me relaxed better than any medicine.

Meet my friends

When I got up in the morning I found Angela sleeping beside me, completely naked. I remembered her kindhearted works, I touched her beautiful face. She was really pretty and attractive. It is true that 'a pretty girl is prettier when she sleeps'. A little later she opened her eyes and said morning. I had stared at her beauty.

- 'What happened?", she asked with a surprise.

- "Nothing! Thanks for last night. Oh! It has been a long time I have no news from Ramiz and his friends. If it is okay with you I want to go and see them. If you want, make some ropes".

-"It is clear that you are still drunk and dizzy. Why do you want to see them? They make trouble for us", she said.

I kissed her forehead and said "Somewhere I read 'Those who wreak are happy for one day, and those who forgive; forever'". But she shook her head and left the room without any words.

Before leaving the camp, I went to see Jim. He had made a place beside the goats fold to put his wine vats to be safe of Ramiz and his friends' robberies. Demet was busy of spinning in the fold. She looked at me with a grin and said "I see the lover pigeon is going out alone. Is there any problem? Maybe the female pigeon has laid eggs and has slept in them!" and she laughed a lot. I thought Demet was cheeky because I had been very kind to her. I knew that her words were due to her jealous feeling, but I could not stand anymore, I must do something. Though I did not say anything and with a fake smile I pretended I had not understood anything about her words. I decided to do something to make her stop this rudeness. With a straw hat that Angela had made,

Jim was helping Demet. I asked his favor to give me a wine vat for my friends. He looked at me friendly and said "As Plato says 'there are two forces in the world: sword and wisdom, yet most of the time this is the sword that wins the wisdom'", then he gave me a wine crock. I was glad of his favor and I left the camp happily. On the way I thought I should have lunch with them so I hunted some birds as well.

It was noon when I arrived at the west bank of the island. Everywhere was calm. Several months had passed, but there was nothing new to attract attention. I think that time the book "Who stole my cheese?" had not been published or it was possible my friends read it and do something to save their life. I approached the cave, nobody was there. Beside the entrance there was a stack of oyster, I thought how it was possible they fish all these oysters. When I entered into the cave, it seemed they were busy dividing something as they tried to pretend there was nothing however their behavior was friendly. Seeing them in those cloths made me laugh as I thought I had passed back to the prehistoric period and there were some Neanderthal human beings in front of me. I went closer and greeted with them. I threw the hunted birds in front of them and said "If you wish, I want to be together like the old days, to eat and drink, to chat a little, I have brought wine as well". Their looking's at the birds made it clear that it was a long time they had not tasted meat. Reza was annoyed, perhaps due to his previous behavior, but Hakan and Ramiz were too happy that they never wanted to cancel a delicious lunch. Ramiz looked at Hakan seriously and with a head gesture asked him to make the birds ready for lunch. When Hakan left us, Ramiz touched his nasty dirty beard and said "It is nice to meet you. We have a difficult life here, and if we continue this way we will have malnutrition. If we had a friendly behavior with you we could have a good and enjoyable life on this island". Reza was looking down and busy with some little stones. I asked Ramiz to send Reza to be with Hakan so we could talk privately. When Reza left us I told Ramiz "I see you are still waiting for relief occult. How long do you want to be lazy and lose the time? Have you forgotten what we were doing in our office? Where are those innovations?". He shook his head and drinking a little wine he said "How? We don't have even a knife?".

-"So the prehistoric people were more intelligent than you. They were making ax, hammer, sword and lance by cutting stones. God Damn you! You have not even made wooden bow and arrows to hunt birds. I don't know how attractive here is that you prefer living here to leaving", I said.

Scratching his hair in a disgusting way he said "So what should we do now?".

- "I have found an old cottage in the jungle, seems nobody has lived there for a long time. I found some useful carpentry tools there too. We can all make a big ship to leave here", I replied.

He thought for a while and said "I don't dare! I can't swim in an ocean that most of the time is stormy. Meanwhile, I have the experience of facing the sharks when the plane crashed down. I never want to have the same story. But I will talk to my friends, perhaps conditionally they would help you in making the ship. We will announce the result up to tomorrow afternoon".

I accepted and said "If there is nobody to help me, I will make the ship and leave here to bring rescue team, but if I have assistants, the ship will be stronger and we will get the result as soon as possible".

A few minutes later, Hakan and Reza entered the cave with grilled meat and we were all together and passed enjoyable time. They were eating with greedy taste and I was filling their wine glasses that were some broken coconut peel. I pretend to drink a little as I feared the white powder I had poured into the wine would affect me too and I would go into a deep sleep. After the lunch they felt sleepy. Hakan was completely drunk and after the last drinking, he stood up and said "I drink this last wine for "Ramiz", the richest man of the island". I was astonished to hear that and waited to see what the matter was. Had they found out something secretly. I asked Hakan "Have you found a treasure?". He smiled and looked at Ramiz, he wanted to say something, but he asked him to be silent. I was sure they had a secret so without attracting their attention I filled their wine bowls to make them lose their control as much as possible and talk about their secret. Reza was a little bit drunk and started loud laughing and said "I have found as much as Ramiz. I don't know how many they are but there are many. This time when I go to the sea I know where I should go to...". Suddenly I remembered the seashells in front of the cave. They had hunted pearl. I laughed at them and thought how poor they were to be happy about those little things. I was sure whatever they found was unworthy comparing with our treasure. After half an hour they were completely unconscious. I decided to come to the camp. I wanted to leave the cave that I got an idea. I took a bunch of the pearl out of their pockets. To make the scene more interesting, I put Reza's hand in Ramiz's pocket to fight with each other whenever they got up.

It was evening when I arrived at the camp. Angela had made a fire out of the camp and was waiting for me. Seeing me she ran towards and hugged me. Her eyes revealed her keen to see me. I kissed her and we both entered the camp. After dinner, I told the story that I had met my friends.

-"What do you think about their conditions?" Jim asked.

-"I don't know. Maybe they want some of the goats, or to stay in the camp or some guns", I said. Suddenly I remembered Demet's joshes and to retaliate it, I said with a serious tone "or as they have been far from their families for a long time, maybe they want Demet as a reward and we have to accept". With this sentence everybody laughed at Demet and she got red and said "Who knows maybe they want Angela".

- " Everybody knows that this pretty pigeon is always and everywhere with her partner. They want a wild single deer that prefer to meet her partner secretly behind the bushes", I said.

Demat was astonished to hear these words and got it that I had known her secret meeting with Hakan. So she did not say anything and went to her room angrily. At midnight when we wanted to go to our room, Angela was talking about Demet and how she got embarrassed. Before sleeping, I showed Angela the bag full of pearls.

-"Where did you get them from?" she asked with a surprise.

-"This is a gift from Ramiz and his friends to apologize us for all their bad works. Of course they did not give it directly. No! I got everything from their eyes and by the help of your amazing powder I actualized their dreams", I said with a righteous looking. We both laughed.

That night I thought a lot about the conditions probably Ramiz and his friends could bring up. They suffered from lack of food and shelter and if they wanted to ask some things for eating or somewhere to live I could accept. I was not sure how many men wanted to come with me and what would happen for those who preferred to stay. I was sure of Angela, I knew that wherever I go that crazy girl would follow me. But about Demet and Jim I did not know what to do. Although they should think about their life, I was worried that Ramiz and his friends would bother them, especially as Demet and Hakan had a secret relationship. That night I dreamed that Ramiz and his friends were taking Demet and Angela with themselves and I run after them but I could not catch them. Suddenly I screamed and got up. Angela had hugged me in her arms and had slept. I kissed her and slept calmly.

See a ship

The next day I was waiting for a message from Ramiz and I could not leave the camp. Angela and Jim were busy making clay dishes. Demet had taken the goats out of the camp. I was sure she was annoyed of the last night talking and did not want to see me. It was eleven, I was out of mood and decided to go fishing. I took my lances and went to the wharf. Demet had sat down under a tree at the beach and was blowing her fife. Seeing me she frowned and turned her face, but I approached her and sat beside her. It was clear that she did not want to talk to me. I thought a while and said "I did not want to bother you last night. And if you want to be sure I should tell that even Angela does not anything about this issue. Here you can live the way you prefer, but I don't like anybody to be scandalized. I felt you poke your nose in an affair that you don't have any information and you should stop it". She looked at me and without saying anything she turned her head. She was a little bit persuaded so I could go on the talking. So I said "today I got a time to live for myself away from that crazy girl and I want to swim". There I took off my cloth and jumped into the sea, then I came back and said "oh! You said you are not good at swimming, if you want I can teach you". It was a long time since I had gone swimming with Angela and this time it was really enjoyable, the gulf water was so clean that I could see the fish and sand of the sea floor. A little bit later, Demet jumped into the sea, she approached me and with a smile she said "of course I did not mean I don't know how to swim, I have just problems

In breathing". Then she started to splash the water to show her swimming. When she got tired, she stopped and asked "How was it?".

-"Really interesting! You swim exactly like a lizard", I said seriously.

-"Really?", she asked happily.

- "Yes! Lizards struggle in the water and then they are sunk", I said and laughed.

   She laughed as well and splashed water on me. I went closer to her and explained about the way of the standard movement of hands and legs during swimming. Then I asked her to put her stomach on my hands and execute the movements I had explained. At first she was in doubt, but when she looked around to be sure nobody watching us, she laid on my hands and started to swim. She was a smart girl and in a few minutes she had learnt "breast stroke" principles. After an hour practice, she was swimming correctly; she did not believe that she had learnt quickly. Getting tired, she stopped and kissed me happily. I looked at her beautiful eyes, I felt that there was a mermaid in front of me. She wanted to kiss me again when we heard a cough. Ramiz and his friends were at the beach and watching us curiously. We came out of the water and I approached them. Demet did not like their sensual looks so she hurried to wear her clothes. When I went closer I saw that Reza's eye was bruised, I knew that my plan had worked and they had fought each other.

-"So what did you decide finally? Did you make any decision?", I asked Ramiz with a smile.

- "You know I believe that Noah lived for a long time as he had pretty wives and enjoyable life. I don't know why you want to leave here?", Ramiz said looking at Demet. Then he pointed to Demet that was wearing her clothes and continued, "With this joyful heavenly life you have made for yourself here, you can live for a hundred years".

- "It does not matter to me. I can make a heaven for myself wherever I go. I want to leave this heaven for the sake of my family, but I am curious why you don't want to leave this hell you have made for yourselves", I said.

Meanwhile, Demet wanted to take the goats to the camp, she had to pass us so she waved to me. Seeing I was swimming with Demet, Hakan was a little irritated. He frowned and said "we stand this hell to hope to reach a heaven. Be sure when we come back to our homeland, we are rich enough to make a heaven for ourselves".

- "Maybe by selling a few pearls, isn't it?", I said while laughing.

- "How do you know?", Reza asked with a surprise.

- "Yesterday you drank so much that you told everything", I replied.

Hearing this Ramiz was very annoyed and shouted "You crazy men! Go to hell! I don't want to see you anymore". When they left us, Ramiz shook his head and said "With these dunce men, hell is too much for us". He got a deep breath and said "we will help you to make the ship but we have some conditions. First of all, during making the ship we will live with you in this camp and you have to share your food with us too. Second, when the ship is ready, if all of you want to leave the island, we will get all the reminded things and the camp; however, if anybody of you wants to stay here, we will take half of the goats, two rifles and some bullets".

- "Okay!", I smiled and said.

He wanted to shake hands with me when Hakan and Reza run towards us while they were shouting "A ship! A ship!". I looked at the sea and saw a big ship was coming towards the island. I was very happy. Ramiz and his friends were happy and hugged each other, they were jumping up and down. He was crying of happiness and said "You see, I had told you they would come to save us. Thanks God!". Then he cleaned his tears and said "we should go to collect our stuff, tonight we will have dinner on the deck".

A few minutes later after they left there, Angela rushed towards me, she was worried and panting. Without any words, she delivered me the binoculars, two rifles and some bullets she had brought. The ship was near the gulf mouth and seemed it wanted to moor there. I watched over with the binoculars, it was not like fishing ships. At first, I did not notice anything special, but when I looked carefully I did not see any flag. The sailors were busy on the deck and they wanted to put two of the boats into the water. Putting her hand on my shoulder, Angela said "Yahsar! I think they are pirates". I nodded my head and said "Maybe!". When I was doing military service in the navy, I had learnt that when a ship enters a country's territory, it must raise its flag to be recognized even the ship belongs to that country. Jim and Demet joined us too.

-"I feel bad, their ship does not look like a rescue ship, its nationality is not clear; I am not sure they are here to save use", Jim said.

-"Surely they have noticed our presence by the clay furnace smoke", Angela said.

- "What should we do now?", Demet asked with a worried voice.

I watched them again with the binoculars. The boats were on the water and each of them was carrying four paddling sailors and two others who were watching around with binoculars.

-"I think it is an easy case. We hide behind the trees and shot air gunshots, if they do the same it means they sign us and they are here to rescue us, but if they shoot us it is clear that they are pirates', I said.

- "Maybe they are smarter than us and know our trick", Angela said.

- "If they were intelligent, they would never be pirates", I said.

We hid quickly behind the trees. Angela gave one of the rifles to Jim and shot some air gunshots with my gesture. Immediately the men in the boat lay on the boat and they shot towards the beach. Although none of the bullets hit us, I was right and I saw how my friends were looking at me astonished. They shot a little bit and when they saw no response from us, they thought they had killed us or we had escaped so they started paddling to the beach. I took the rifle from Angela and asked her to go with Demet to the camp to send all the bullets we had by Demet. She herself had to go the ammunition store to bring us rifles and bullets. When the girls left us I told Jim, "Are you ready for the tourney? The right boat for me, let me see how many of them you can shoot". And we started shooting. Jim began first, although he was old, I could see with the binoculars that how he shot one of the sailors in the left boat with his first shot. The attackers who did not expect this reaction from us shot as quickly as they could, but as the boats were moving they failed in their shots. Before Demet could join us, we had killed three armed men and two sailors so that they had to come back to their ship. After a few minutes we unbelievably heard the roaring of the cannons. "Lay down", Jim shouted. Demet and I jumped into a pit near there, then after everywhere was full of fire and smoke. They shot ten cannons to different parts of the island, three of them hit the beach, but there was no problem for us. Then they shot the beach heavily with a machine gun. I looked at Jim with a surprise and said "Damn! They have everything, what should we do now?" Pressing his teeth angrily, Jim said "Tonight we will teach them a lesson". The shooting had been stopped and I was worried about Angela and other friends, Ramiz and his friends were behind the bushes, they joined us secretly. They were completely shocked by what had happened and asked what we should do.

- "We should be ready for a big battle", I said.

- "With a few old rifles, do you want to fight with a big artillery?", Ramiz asked.

- "What do you think? We have too much ammunition that we can exterminate twenty ships like that", I said.

Everybody looked at Jim with a surprise and he confirmed me without understanding anything of our talking. Then he looked at me and asked "What is your plan?".

-"I have not a special plan. I think we should wait for their reaction", I said.

He shook his head and said "No! No! Go to the ammunition store and bring mortars and grenades. I want to put them in three corners of the gulf and we will shoot at them from three corners when it is dark".

- "Shouldn't we capture the ship safely", I asked.

-"Do you have an idea?" he asked.

-"Maybe we could do something", I replied.

- "Okay! You should go to bring the ammunitions and I will watch them over. If they want to come to the beach, I will shoot them. Now hurry up!", Jim said. It was an interesting idea and we all rushed towards the camp.

It was three in the afternoon when we arrived at the camp. Two of the cannons had hit the camp; and the gate and Jim's cottage had been collapsed. Angela joined us, she had brought four binoculars, three rifles and two hundred fold boxes of bullets. The guys were astonished to see all those ammunitions but I was more astonished that how a tiny girl could carry all these things to the camp. Anyway, each of them took a rifle and checked it, they got more astonished when they knew that all of them belonged to the Second World War. The camp was not safe anymore as it was seen easily from the gulf and they may blast it again. So we moved towards the ammunitions store.

An hour later we were near the crashed plane and took out the ammunitions from subsoil. Seeing all those stuffs, Ramiz and his friend were amazed. Ramiz told me "Yashar! I was wrong about you, you ...., you are really....". He kissed my hands and cried. I took his arms and said "Don't be sad! We are friends and we should not be offended of each other". Then I took his shoulders and said "Men do not cry". I kissed him and we began to take whatever we needed of the ammunitions.

We took what we wanted, then buried all the others and started to plan the battle strategy. Ramiz was a very proficient at swimming, he said "At night I will swim to the ship and attach some grenades to its propeller, so when it wants to move it will be exploded and sank". His suggestion was not interesting as I wanted to take the ship as safe as possible.

-"When I was doing military service in the army, I knew how to work with a mortar. If we don't want to explode the ship, what will we do with these things?", Hakan said.

- "We can stop their movement to the beach", I said.

- "If they want to do so, be sure we will react against them with mortars', Reza said.

- "If their cannons will not work anymore", I said. They looked at me with a surprise.

-"Tonight I will swim to the ship and if I can go to the deck, with some grenades I will make their cannons and machine gun out of work", I said.

- "I will come with you, I had been in the army and I know something about the battle. This time I will never leave you and I will be with you even if the end is death", Ramiz said.

Putting my hand on his shoulder, I said "So up to the evening we will make a Braque and will go towards the ship after it gets dark".

Feeling stressful, Reza said "And then?".

- "When we are close to the ship, Ramiz and I will go into the water and swim to the ship and clime the anchor rope", I continued.

-"So what will we do?", Angela asked.

'You, Demet and Jim will go to the north rocks of the island where we hunted the sharks. After the explosion of the grenades, you will shoot the ship to attract their attention to yourselves while Ramiz and I will shoot those who are on the deck", I replied.

- "What will I do then?", Hakan asked.

- "You should stay at the beach and support us if it is needed, if our plan fails, maybe we have to react with mortars", I said.

- "What if they surround and capture you?", Demet said.

Looking at Angela, I said "Then you should write on our gravestone 'Here is the grave of a hero'" and we all laughed. Angela was upset by my words, she hugged me and said "Damn! I am stressful, why do you say this?". I laughed and said "Don't worry! Before they capture us, we will jump into the water and will come to the beach by the Braque".

-"Yashar! Promise to come back safe", she whispered to me while she was crying.

-"Be sure! I will come back safe, the legends will never die", I said while kissing her.

That day we made the Braque and carried the ammunitions to the beach until the afternoon without attracting the pirates' attention and then we hid behind the trees and waited for night. My friends were all there; stress and worry were seen on their faces. I stood up and said "My friends, I never fear of death as all people who know me even my wife and son think that I have died, this helps me to accept danger with ease. But be sure that we will be the winner of the battle and will overcome this problem like the other ones. We have been created for victory, we don't know the meaning of failure.....". When I finished my speech, I could see that all of my friends were so excited that even the most timid member of the group, Reza, was ready to fight, he pressed his teeth and said "I want to swim to the ship and kill them all with a fist!". We all laughed by his words. I felt joyful to see the friendship among the men, they had all forgotten the disputes and their only challenge was to kill the enemy.

The far-reaching end

Jim and the girls started their way before the sunset to reach the northern rocks of the island which was very close to the pirates 'ship. They should wait for our sign. Before going, Angela took me in her arms in the presence of everybody and kissed my face and whispered to me "Yashar! I know you welcome the danger, but let me come with you instead of Reza. I want to be with you even at the time of death". I took her head with my hands and said "What do you mean? Which danger? Which death? We will destroy the enemy in a few hours and come back safe". She smiled and followed Jim and Demet to the forest.

When it got dark, I recommended the last points to Hakan and put the Braque to the water. Ramiz and I had sat on the one side of the Braque and paddling quietly. Holding a rifle, Reza had sat between us and was looking around anxiously. Although we had rubbed coal on our faces not to be seen, I could see how he had been frightened and trembling with fear. I whispered to him, "What is up Man!? What do you fear from?".

- "Maybe some men come out of water in a minute and shoot us?", he said with a trembling voice.

- "If they knew that there is a brave man like you here, they would surely do this. Hey man, did not you do the military service? Why do you fear?", I said while laughing.

-"Why not, he did, but all the time he had been in the garrison kitchen with onions and potatoes!", Ramiz said quietly.

-"I want to admit something, but promise never laugh at me later. To be honest, I fear death. I don't want to die in a dark night, I....", Reza said.

"You stupid! I fear too, but not as much as you. Control you not to make a mistake.", Ramiz said.

-"Do you know why Alexander the Macedonian was successful? He always believed that the enemy is like a sheep herd and he was telling his soldiers 'A butcher does not fear from a big amount of sheep'. Don't fear! We have saved ourselves from the plane crash and be sure we will overcome this problem with ease", I said.

When we arrived in a hundred meter distance of the ship we put down the paddles and controlled the situation with the binoculars. There were two men on the deck. One of them was walking around the cannon, the other one was at the other end of the ship, where there was the machine gun. The way they were walking and smoking showed that they were not in a good mood and we could destroy them easily. Before we jumped into the water I recommended the last points to Reza and asked her to wait for our signal for shooting. The farewell moment was hard, we greeted the friends and jumped into the water with tearful eyes. Each of us had three grenades and a rifle, we had taken them out of the water not to be wet. Swimming was difficult in that situation, especially when we were stressful as well. I had learnt all the principles of entering the ship of the enemy and capturing it when I was in the navy. So I climbed the anchor rope and went to the deck secretly. The man near the cannon was an amateur sailor and I killed him easily. I pulled his corpse behind a box not to be seen, then I pointed to Ramiz to climb the anchor. When he came, I asked him to care me as I wanted to kill the guard and the machine gun to destroy both of them, but Ramiz stopped me and said we should do this by grenades. Although it was easy for me to cover my own plan, I wish I had not listened to Ramiz. The machine gun was in a place that they could not shoot us, so I pulled the hand grenade and threw it inside the cannon. It was blasted with such a fearsome sound that I felt the ship trembling. I did not expect a grenade belonging to fifty years ago have such a powerful sound. The explosion of the cannon made all the sailors worried, the guard of the machine gun together with some others ran towards the front of the ship and began to shoot us. At first we threw some grenades to them, but unbelievably they were not exploded. I guessed they were linden so we took our rifle and started shooting them. We could hear shooting sound from where Angela and Jim were. Reza, also, had begun shooting without our signal. Surrounded from everywhere, the sailors were confused for a while, but then one of them approached to the machine gun and began shooting to the rocks where Angela and Jim were there and to the Braque where Reza had hidden himself. Then there was no reaction from our friends, I had a bad feeling, I thought they had all been killed. Ramiz was more stressful than me, he pulled the hand grenades and threw them one by one towards the pirate while he was shouting "Damn! Damn!". Two of them blasted and killed a few of the pirates. He wanted to throw the last grenade when one of the injured pirates shot him in his chest. When I saw this scene and the blood on his chest I did not understand anything. I came out from behind the box and without caring their shooting, I moved towards the pirates while I was shouting with irritation. My right leg was shot, but I was so wroth that I could not feel any pain. I was moving forward and shooting, I was killing them one by one. I wanted to kill until to be killed. I was feeling that my life was worthless when they had killed my friends. The last person I killed was the man who had shot my friends with the machine gun. Killing him everywhere was in silence. The room of the captain was on fire due to the blast of the grenades and the flames were getting more and more. I could not do anything more and I had to leave the ship. I came back to Ramiz to take him when I found him alive. I was very happy to see this and I took his head in my arms. He had lost lots of blood and there was no hope for his life. His eyes were semi- opened, he coughed a little and then said "Yashar! Could you destroy all of them?". I nodded while I was crying. "Well done! You are really a professional butcher and you never fear of the sheep", he said with a smile. He asked about Reza and other friends. "They fought bravely and all of them are waiting for us at the beach now, you fought well and we are proud of you, now we will go to the beach and celebrate this victory with our friends", I said while I was crying. He coughed again and said "Yahsar! I am going to die, I have just a request, please forgive me, never tell my family that I was a bad man and made problems for you, please". He said this and closed his eyes forever. I pressed his head to my chest and screamed "Oh God!" and cried a lot. That was a really hard time, I kissed his forehead and while I was crying hard I said "I wish you knew I have forgotten you long time ago".

Little by little the sound of explosions from the ship was heard and I had to leave the ship as soon as possible. I took Ramiz corpse and jumped into the water. When I came to the water surface, everywhere was dark and just a little light from the fired ship deck had made the water surface light. I had to find the Braque soon as the blood from my body and Ramiz's corpse had spread into the water and it could attract the sharks. I called Reza several times, but there was no reply. I had kept Ramiz's corpse on the water surface and I was swimming to find out the Braque when there was a big explosion of the pirates' ship and it got fired completely. Under the light of the ship I could see the Braque. I swam to it. When I got it, I could not see Reza, but his rifle was in it. Immediately I got in the Braque and pulled the corpse into it. I watched around well and called Reza again, but there was no answer, I could not see anything in the water either. I thought he was frightened and had jumped into the water to swim to the beach. So I paddle with the butt stock to the beach. It was midnight when I arrived at the beach. None of my friends were at the beach. I was very tired and putting the corpse down I laid down there, and looking at the fired ship of the pirates I got sleep.

The next day morning, it was sunny and the sea was calm. Burning wounds remind me the events of the last night and I saw the corpse of Ramiz beside me. The pirates" ship. I stood up and looked around. There was neither a corpse nor my friends. I did not know what had happened to them. I dressed my wounds with a piece of my cloth and though it was very painful, I buried Ramiz there with lots of crying. Farewell to him was very hard for me, then after I sat down beside his grave and thought why it ended like that. I wished I had not listened to Ramiz and I should do the work myself. That moment I felt really lonely like the day I had arrived at the island on the first day. The sea was very calm as if those events had not happened last night. I listened to the waves, they calmed me in a strange way and I felt they were telling me "Forget the past and think about the future. The passed time will never come back".

I was thinking when I heard Angela from far distance. I stood up and I saw her that had come out of the forest and was coming towards me. Behind her there were Hakan, Demet and Jim. Hakan was carrying Jim on his back and Demat was limping. Apparently both of them had been injured. I waved Angela, she saw me and ran towards me. I limped a few steps too. When we joined each other, she hugged me in a way as if it was so many years we were far from each other. She was crying and saying some things in her mother tongue. I cleaned her tears and said

"I am happy you are still alive". She kissed my hands and said "My dear Yahsar! You don't know how much I prayed God to keep you safe. I wished I had died, but you were not injured". She hugged me again and started crying.

A little bit later the other friends came as well and we sat under a tree. Demet had sprained her leg in the rocks. It was painful, but it was not very important. But Jim had been shot in both his legs. He had serious wounds, but Angela had cured them with a proper ointment.

- "Why did you leave your position? I had told you to support us with the mortars. Didn't you think if we could not be successful, it was your duty to blast the beach. We were lucky that the cannon were out of work otherwise they had destroyed all parts of the island", I told Hakan.

- "I was worried about my friends and I wanted to help them. I knew I was wrong, but when I saw they shot them with the machine gun I thought I should go, so I joined them in the darkness", feeling ashamed of his work, he said and looked at Demet. When Demet saw her lover had done such a risky work she smiled.

- "What about Ramiz and Reza? I can't see them!", Jim asked.

- "I don't know anything about Reza. Maybe he had been shot last night, but Ramiz......", I said.

-"What has happened for Ramiz?", Hakan asked with a worried voice.

- "Ramiz fought valiantly and was killed to save our lives", I said, touching his grave which was under the same tree. Hakan had a strong friendship relation with Ramiz so he touched the grave and started crying. I could not stand it, I stood up and said "I want to walk around the beach maybe I could find Reza". Angela stood up too, and getting my waist said "The loved pigeons will never be alone". I kissed her forehead and we left there.

We walked around the gulf edges and a part of the west bank of the island until noon, but we could not find out anything, neither Reza and nor pirates and their ships. Although Angela was beside me all the time whispering love in my ears, I was confused by the end of the story happened last night, so I was not in a good mood. I was angry because we wanted to be successful and if we were a little bit careful, we would get the best result. I was hatred and if Angela was not beside me, I would sit down there and cried a lot. The wind started to blow and the sea was raging. The gray sky was the sign of a heavy rain and we had to come back to the camp as soon as possible.

On the way to the camp, we arrived at the west part of the gulf when it started to rain heavily. Although we had taken some big leaves over our head as an umbrella we were completely wet. Little by little I felt cold and started shivering. When we arrived at the camp, I was completely tired and could not move anymore. Angela went into the bower and called me to join her. I stood for a while and looked at the destroyed gate of the camp. I remembered how hard we worked to make it, my heart was beating fast and I was panting. I felt a pain in my head, so strong that I could not hear anything more. Angela asked me to join her, but after a few steps I fell down.

Beautiful dream

When I opened my eyes, I found myself in a big beautiful garden with lots of birds. I had no pain in my head and I did not feel cold. I was strangely happy. I did not know where I was but it was enjoyable. I called Angela and other friends, but none of them were there. I was walking among the beautiful trees and plants that I had never seen before. Touching all the trees and plants I had a great feeling. It was a strange experience because touching them all my senses could feel enjoyment. The most enjoyable part of the story was that all these enjoy were different from one another. When I was touching something I could feel its sound, smell and taste. Then from a far distance, I heard the voice of two men laughing; then I moved towards them. I thought I knew them, I saw Ramiz and Reza had sat down beside a river stream and were talking. I joined them. Their smiles and looks revealed that they were happy about their new life. I looked at them with a surprise and asked "I looked for you for a long time! Where were you? Where is here? Where are the others?". "They are waiting for you. Don't leave them alone!", Ramiz said with a kindhearted look. Then he touched my face. I woke up of dream. I had sweated. Angela was cleaning my face. She looked down and said "Thanks God! Finally, he got his conscious!" I looked around and found myself lying on the bed with just underwear. The room was full of herbs. I could smell a strange smoke in the room. Maybe Angela had made it to disinfect the room. It was too hot inside that even she had got her underwear's only, she was making drug for me. There were lots of strange plants and if her skin was black I would think that an African wizard was taking care of me. She came closer and gave me some herbal juice. It was so bitter that in a moment I vibrated and bristled my hair. She measured my heart beat and said "Well! You are okay!".

- "What happened? Where are the others?", I asked.

- "They are all good. They have gone to the forest to bring bamboo to repair the gate and Jim's room", she said with a smile.

- "What is up? What happened?", I asked with a surprise. She came and sat down beside my bed. Touching my face, she said " You have cold for a few days, lying unconscious on the bed and saying delirium. Do you remember anything about the pirates attack?".

Suddenly I remembered the scene when Ramiz was shot on the deck and then the whole of the story came to my mind. I stood up, getting my head in my hands, I was walking in the room.

-"You are not okay yet, you should take a rest!", Angela told me.

-"Did you find Reza's corpse?", I asked.

-"Yes, we did! But how do you know that he died", she asked me.

- "Maybe you don't believe, but I saw them walking in the heaven", I replied.

-"In the heave?! They are not permitted to enter the hell even", she said while laughing. Then she gave me a piece of his cloth with a pocket on it. It was clear that he had been attacked by the sharks. Inside the pocket there was a photo of him and his family, taken before our travel. I sat by the bed and looking at the photo I cried.

- "Maybe he was injured in the shooting and then fell down into the sea. May rest in peace. God knows how a hard death he had", she said.

-"Believe me, I saw them in the heaven. They sacrificed themselves to save our life", I said. That day I took a rest in bed as Angela had recommended and took the medicine she had made of the strange plants and herbs. She took care of me in all those days. I thought besides the medicine she had given me something else, as I had fallen in her love and I could not stand to be far from her even for a while.

The next day I woke up with a good feeling. Angela was still sleeping. She had taken care of me for the last few days and was tired, so I did not want to wake her up. I kissed her forehead and I left the room. Everybody was sleeping, so I got a time to walk around the camp and renew the memories. There were lots of cut bamboo pieces. They were clearly for repairing the camp, but while Jim had injured his legs, which had brought all these. A little while Demet came out of her room.

- "Hi Man! I am happy to see you good. We all prayed for your health. If you were not brave, who knew what had happened to us!....", she said seeing me.

I interrupted her words and said "You did your best as well. Everybody played a role in this victory. And who had brought all these bamboos?".

- "Hakan! He is very interested in living in the camp and with us. He has promised to repair all the destroyed parts of the camp by himself. But Jim suggested him to wait until you were good to ask your opinion too. After all, you are the mayor of the camp", Demet replied.

- "Well! Where is he now?", I asked.

- "He has made a shelter behind the bamboos for himself. He is sleeping there.", she said with a smile.

- "Why does not he stay with the wild deer?", I asked while laughing.

She felt shy, looked down and said that she should milk the goats and makes the breakfast ready. She added that everybody would be happy to see me; and she ran towards the fold.

Up to breakfast time, I went to see Ramiz's grave. It was astonishing to see many candles my friends had burned in the memory of his soul. Remembering all good times we had in our office, I got depressed. I sat down there and cried. A little while Angela came and sat beside me.

- "I am sure they are in the heaven. They were real heroes", she said, touching my head. She took my hand and we came back to the camp.

That day we had a great breakfast. We were all happy to be together again. After the breakfast, Hakan stood up and said "Yahsar! I apologize for all my misbehavior. I want to live here if you let me, of course".

I raised my head and said "Angela had written a good sentence over the gate, do you remember? If you don't deserve, please don't enter. We had tested you once".

He felt shy hearing me and looked down.

-"But I don't think that you don't deserve. We will give one more chance", I added.

-"Thank you. I will start my work today", he said with a smile.

Everybody was happy and clapped. I stood up and thanked my friends for their affection; then I said "as you know I have found some carpentry tools in the ruined old cottage in the forest. I want to make a ship to leave here".

- "Do you mean the cottage belonged to the old woman? Angela has told us the whole of the story", Demet said.

I looked at Angela with a surprise. She looked up and said "After the storm of that day, we found some corpses by the beach. One of them was the man, Saleh, the old lady had talked about before. I suggested to bury him by his mother". Then she looked at me innocently and said "I think you would do the same thing we did, if you were us". I nodded my head and said "You did well. We should go and meet them". We both left the camp.

They had buried Saleh beside his mother and in a view to the sea. I was sure that their soul had rested in peace. Although he and his friends had caused I lost two of my friends, I had no bad feeling to Saleh. I was not sure, maybe as we had killed all of them, or perhaps it was due to the treasure her mother had gifted us generously. But I felt that I was still owed to the old woman; and her husband should be buried beside them. First of all, we brought the jewels out of the cave and hid in a part of the forest, then we transformed Faroogh's corpse beside his family. We wanted to keep the treasury safe and find it with ease next time. I wanted to hide the whole of it in a part of the forest and then deliver it to the Indonesia government after leaving the island, but Angela said we should hide it in two different parts of the island. I did not find any reason for this decision. I asked her and she said "Since I have gotten familiar with you, I have learned to do something that shows its effects later on. So don't ask anything right now". We then brought the corpses out of the cave; we buried Faroogh's corpse beside his family, and the corpse belonging to the Japanese soldier by the crashed plane and beside his friends. I was sure that their souls were in peace so I had a good feeling. At the same time Hakan, Jim and Demet had repaired the destroyed part of the camp. Then Hakan got the permission to stay in the camp. After a few says of working, one night I stood up after the dinner and said "I will start making the ship seriously from tomorrow. Although I know you enjoy living in here I hope you will help me to finish the work as soon as possible. I don't want to wait for help anymore".

- "How do you know we don't want to come with you? I have changed my idea and want to follow you", Demet said. She looked at Hakan to know his idea too. Hakan did not expect Demet to leave the island, he got confused and said "Of course, I follow the others. Whatever you say!". We all looked at Jim. He drank his wine glass and said "I will give you the best of my wine, although I don't come with you, whenever you drink it you will remember me". Then he looked down.

-"Do you have any plan to make a ship for four persons?", Angela asked.

- "If we work seriously, we can make Noah ship as well", I said nodding, and we all laughed.

It was midnight and the moon was shining in the sky. Angela was beside me like a pretty mermaid. I explained about the details of the ship I was going to make when she put his finger on my lips and said "Why didn't you ask me anything about the travel? Are you sure I will come with you?".

- "You are a part of my life now!", I said while kissing her finger which was still on my lips.

She looked down and said with a depressed voice "But you....".

-"But what?", I asked.

She paused and said "You have your own family. When we leave here, you will live with them".

I sat down beside the bed, she was right, but I had fallen in love with her, I could not stand losing her. I looked up and asked God to show me a good solution.

Build the ship

The next day in the morning, I went to the forest together with Jim and Hakan to cut the trees to make the ship. On the way to the forest Jim and Hakan were worried about the way we could carry the big trees to the beach. They were right as even if we were strong enough physically, we could not transport them among all those plants and bushes. But I had thought about the solution. To do the work with ease we went to the forest on the northern heights of the island. There was a headland in the west part towards the gulf. We could cut the trees and throw them into the gulf, the waves could carry them to the beach. This was the solution I had learned from one of my friends working in a sawmill. If we threw the timbers into the sea at noon, probably the waves would move them far away from the beach so we waited for the sea tide until the afternoon to bring at least two or three of the timbers to the beach. Although it was time consuming and tiring, it was not too hard. We cut about seven trees until the afternoon and threw them into the sea and came back to the camp.

We arrived at the camp before the sunset. The girls were busy making the ropes out of barks in front of the camp gate. They got astonished when they saw us without the timbers.

- "You look as a failed army! What about the timbers?", Demet asked.

- "Tomorrow they will arrive!", I said.

- "Maybe with a registered mail, isn't it?", she asked while laughing.

Angela was looking at me as if she wanted to say that she had believed me. She trusted me. She came closer and with her usual smile got the stuff I had in my hand. She did not care others look and kissed my face and whispered me "She is not serious! I believe in you. Take a rest and I will wake you up when the dinner is ready". I was too tired to reply Demet so nodded Angela and went to my room.

That night everybody had an idea about making the ship, but as I had some experiences in sailing and wooden works I did not accept them. So I stood up and explained about my plan in details, at the end they were all astonished and were thinking about it. We were talking in Turkish and Jim had not understood any words of us. But he stood up and with a wine glass in his hand said "I think Yahsar's plan is complete, I myself want to sail it to America". We all burst into laugh hearing his words.

Tomorrow morning we all went to the beach to take the timbers out of the water. Demet did not expect they would reach there so she was laughing at us, but when we arrived at there we saw six of them. The water had passed away due to the sea tide and the timbers were side by side as if somebody had set them. It was strange, even for me, but I thought they were gifts of God to remind us that he never forgets his creatures.

We carried all the timbers to a proper place at the beach. Then we put three of them in a parallel form and three others on them. The middle timber was around eight meters and the others on both sides were six meters tall. We sharpened their head with an ax and then we started to saw them vertically. I was going to make them empty with an ax and then stick them together. These trunks would be acted like an air case to keep the ship on the water. It was a hard work, especially as the hot and humid weather had made the work slower than before. Angela suggested that we should make a canopy by the bamboos Hakan had brought from the forest. The canopy was going to be made over the trunks to protect us from the sun and rain. It was interesting; like a ship-making workshop.

We were in two groups. Hakan and Jim were in one group, they had to cut the trunks in half. The second group was Angela and I. We had to make the trunks empty. Demet had the same job she had as a flight attendant. When we finished cutting the timbers, it was turn to stick them together. To do so we used of the white algas that were like a stick. Of course Jim helped us to take many wires and metal strips out of the Japanese airplane to tie the trunks together. Before to stick the trunks together we greased inside and outside of them with the shark oil that we used to make candles. These greased trunks could stand against water penetration. The trunks weight was less than before and they could be carried with ease. We tied the trunks with three wooden pieces together and put a vertical timber in the middle of the chassis as a rig. After seventy days of hard working we made the chassis of our ocean-passing ship.

That night was a great one for us as the dream of leaving the island was getting true. Demet suggested to eat dinner in the workshop. We had a great meal. After the dinner, Angela asked " What should we call the ship?". Then everybody said his own suggestion, names like "Sea wolf", "Oranoos", and "Angel" that none of them was accepted. That night it was clear and the moon was shining in the sky. For a moment I looked at the moon reflect on the water, looked very beautiful with wave movement. I stood up and said "I think we should call it Yakamooz, it means the moon reflection on the water". For a few seconds everybody was silent. Jim was filling in the wine glasses. Repeating its name for several times, Jim said "I want all of you to drink for Yakamooz". Meanwhile Demet stood up and began to clap for me and then all others did the same. At that moment, I was happy and wished

Ramiz and Reza were alive as well then we could celebrate this success together.

From the next day morning we started to bring bamboos to the beach to make the deck and other parts of the ship. Like the first time, we cut the bamboos and bowed their heads and ends to make the wall around the deck. Making the deck was not too hard, but it took two months. We used the cloth inside the crashed plane to make the sails. It was not very strong and probably it could not stand against the strong winds, but Demet had a useful suggestion. She had used the goat wools to weave ropes. She suggested to weave a net by the wool rope to sew it to the sails. It was really great. Then it was turn to make a cabin there. But first of all we decided to throw it into the water and sail around the island to find out if there was any problem.

It was the day for testing the ship. We threw the ship in the water and all got into it except Jim. Hakan and Demet did not know swimming well, so they wore life jackets. Inside the ship we had two clay barrels of rain water, some rifles and some food to eat until the afternoon. Of course we were going to take too much food for our main travel and they were all just to test the problems we probably would have during the journey. Before the trip Jim was a little sad with teary eyes. He hugged me and whispered "Although I know we will be together at night I don't know why I feel depressed. Take care of yourself". And following their own customs, he broke a wine bottle when we led the ship in the water.

It was sunny and a little bit windy. My friends were happy when they saw the ship they had built over a long time of hard work was moving slowly with the little breeze. They were listening to me with a strange excitement to do their duties on time. We sailed around the island until the afternoon with happiness, but it became cloudy and the wind was blowing from the north. The sea got stormy and as we were faced with the wind we had to put away the sails and start to paddle to keep the ship in its way. We had arrived at the rocky beach of the island and the waves were moving us to the rocks. A little mistake could lead us to death and lose the ship we had worked on during the last months. Although we had faced with a serious problem, everything was under control and there was no need to be worried. I was sure that with a little precision and speed we could save our lives. So all the time I wanted them to keep calm and paddle as fast as they could. Angela did not fear and was paddling like an experienced sailor; she was laughing at Demet and Hakan who were very worried and frightened. I was laughing at them too. Angela had noticed my laughs and said "If 'Alfred Hitchcock' had used these scenes in one of his films, I am sure the audience would die, not because of the fear but due to laughing", then she started laughing. For a moment a wave hit over our head and Hakan screamed of fear. "We should keep in mind to make a washroom immediately or in the next storm you will wet your pants", Angela said and began to laugh loudly. Finally, we arrived at the beach. Demet and Hakan took their stuff and got off the ship. Angela came to me and said "With this story I think they will never get on the ship again" and she laughed.

That night Jim had made the dinner, eating the food Angela was describing the story we had with a great excitement and bushwhacked Demet and Hakan. Although for the success we had got we were all happy and were laughing, I felt that Demet was a little bit sad. Angela had drunk a lot so she was still telling the day story even at the time of sleeping and laughing. "I think if next time we want to select a name for the ship, Demet will suggest "Torment angel" instead of "Rescue angel". She was talking and laughing, but the only thing I cared was her attractive beauty. That night she was very pretty and I was just looking at her beautiful eyes.

The test trip was very useful as the problems indicated themselves and we found proper solutions. And now it was the turn to make the cabin. We made it big enough to provide a proper place to take a rest and put our stuff. To prevent the rain penetration into the cabin, Jim suggested that we should cover the walls of the room with the metal pieces taken from the Japanese plane. We used the plane's safe glasses for the windows of the room to have a good view of the sea. Finally Angela tied two hammocks to the chassis and the wall of the cabin to take a rest there whenever the sea was calm and enjoyable. The ship was ready; we should make ready the stuff we needed for our journey and wait for the winds.

It took one week to make ready all the things and the food we needed for the journey. Angela was so smart in this duty that I thought I would travel with an experienced sailor. She had thought about all the details of the travel and had predicted the solution for the probable problems. She had made food ready for four persons for two months and all the herbs we might need during this time. Meanwhile, Jim with his experiences from the Vietnam War made us some squibs to fire to signal our presence to other ships we might see on the way. When everything was ready, we decided to talk about the proper time of the travel. That was the twelfth of March. We had lived for one year and seven days on that island compulsory.

Start the journey

That night Demet and Hakan were very silent; they were eating dinner while looking down. I gestured Angela to ask the reason, but she shrugged her shoulders with no idea. After the dinner Demet stood up and looking down, she said "Yashar! There is something... I want to say that ... Actually... If you let me I want to stay here. You saw how fearful I was today. I am not brave enough to come with you". She said this and sat down. I looked at Hakan. As I expected he did not want to leave her there alone. He looked down feeling ashamed and I knew that he would be there too. Jim had announced his decision before that he did not want to join us. Although it was a long time I knew that my friends would not come with me, that night I was annoyed by their words a little bit. I stood up and said "I wish you had said it before to do a little work and make a smaller ship". Then I left the camp and went towards the wharf.

"Yakammoz" had been tied to the wharf base and was going up and down slowly like a baby cradle. I got into it and lay down on one of the hammocks. I was worried and annoyed by my friends. I thought if we were united, we had left the island sooner than that and Ramiz and Reza were alive too. Angela came a little bit later with a wine bottle. When she saw me she came and lay down beside and said "Don't worry! I will come with you". Then she drank a little wine and said "They should go to hell! One Angela will be better than a hundred of them!", and she laughed. That night Angela suggested to sleep there together. Of course she moved too much that I could not sleep and I just looked at the stars.

It was morning when Angela got up and came down the hammock while yawning. She looked around and screamed "The ship rope has been torn…. The island….. We….". It was sunny and I was paddling, I interrupted her and said "don't worry! The rope has not been torn. I myself opened it". But she was still dizzy and had not got what I said. She looked around again with a surprise, she saw there was no island and asked "What do you mean? Where are we now?".

-"It is about six hours we have started our travel", I said.

-"I had lots of things going to take….", she objected.

I interrupted her and said "Don't worry! I have brought all of them". She went into the cabin and when she was sure everything was okay, scratched her head and said "Well, we should say goodbye to them". She got one of the paddles and started. After a while she said "can I ask why we did not tell them? Did you think I would open the rope and launch the ship again?"

-"No! When you got asleep I was awake and thought a lot, about the island, the ship, my friends and whatever they said at dinner. Actually, there was not any incomplete work and I thought we should not stay more than this on the island, we should not waste the time. So I went to the camp, took the stuffs and when I wanted to leave, I thought I should farewell them. They were all sleeping. I kissed them and left something for them as a memory", I said. Then I sighed and said "Farewell is always very hard for me". Angela looked down and continued paddling, but I was sure she did not want to leave the island.

A mild breeze was blowing in the afternoon, but due to the sails the ship was moving fast, so we put aside the paddles and set the sails ropes to keep the ship in north direction. Jim had made a compass by the use of the Japanese crashed plane to use it in the cloudy weather. Of course it was easy to find the way by the sunset and sunrise during the days and stars at nights. I was sure if we moved to the north we could see the cargo ships and they could rescue us. That day Angela got seasick as she had a full stomach of the previous night. Of course, there was no problem since she had the needed herbs. When it was windy, the ship could move up to twelve miles per hour and we hoped the travel ended in less than two weeks. In the first week there was no especial event; just it rained twice that was very interesting for Angela, made her to be very excited.

Day by day Angela changed her behavior and I knew the reason. She was sure that being rescued meant losing me. During the days she was lying in the hammock, eating fruits or blowing her flute without any words; and at nights, she was sleeping soon. She was out of mood and was speaking less than before, even she replied my questions very short and sometimes in her mother tongue that I could not understand anything. Sometimes she was staring at me for a long time that I feared she would have satanic dreams for me. Although I knew in long sea journeys, sailors quarrel with each other due to food shortage or some psychological problems, we had enough food. Yet I tried to watch her not to make a mistake and put us into trouble. I knew she loved me very much and whatever she may do would be due to failure in love. She was right. It was the seventh day of our travel. She was so mysterious that I dreamed she had got a samurai sword, shouting "I will kill you...I will kill you..", while following me.

We started the second week of our journey with a storm, fortunately it was not too hard to damage our ship. We were wandering in the sea until six in the afternoon without any direction. Angela was inside the cabin when she suddenly came out and shouted "I saw a ship" and pointed to a part of the sea; but the waves were too high that we could not see anything. I stared at there for a moment and saw the ship. It was a cargo ship in a two mile distance from our ship. I was sure they would never hear our voices so I hurried into the cabin and took one of the rifles and shot some air gunshots. It was windy and I knew that it would be hard to hear the shot sounds. So I fired one of the squibs that Jim had made. But unexpectedly they passed us slowly with no reaction. I could not accept it, after all these days, a ship passed and nobody saw us, it was probable they had seen us, but due to an improper weather condition they could not help us. I hoped they would inform our position to other ships or rescue groups. But I was annoyed of the storm of that day, I was cussing everything. Angela had never seen my irritation until that day. She was looking at me with a surprise. When I got calm, she took me into the cabin. My hands were shaking. I sat down on the bed and took my head. Angela sat down beside me and touched my hair and said "Don't worry! God knows the best. Be sure we will be rescued. I will bring you a good drink". She stood up and went to the food storage. Then she came back with a drink and stood in front of me, with a naughty smile she said "Drink it, it will make you calm". I did not know what was there inside the drink and I was not in a good mood to ask about. So I got and drank it. I laid down on the bed and was thinking to the ship passed us. Angela came and sat beside me. She was touching me, I felt I was getting numb and unconscious.

- "What was in the drink? I feel sleepy", I asked.

-"That is good. Let me do everything", she said with a smile. Then she touched my eyes and I did not know anything more.

When I opened my eyes the storm had finished. I stood up and went out. It was sunny and Angela was paddling. Seeing me she put aside the paddles and said good morning. I looked around with a strange and asked "What you mean by 'good morning'?".

-"It means you slept until morning", she said with a smile.

At first I did not understand what she meant, but then I remembered what had happened last night and asked her, "Did you pour that white powder into the drink?".

She laughed and nodded. I was angry and wanted to object, but she came closer and hugging me said "last night you were not good. I was worried about you, so I thought that was the best way to make you calm". Taking her arms aside, I shook my head and said "Anyway! You should tell me before. Don't do it again". She looked down and laughed. It was strange for me because whenever I objected her, she used to frown and be annoyed, but this time it was completely the opposite. That day I did not understand anything of that, but later on, after a few months I knew what a mistake she had done.

During the second week of the journey we witnessed several storms. But the last one was so huge that it damaged the chassis of the ship and the roof of the cabin. Then two big waves broke the walls of the cabin and took some of the stuff which was inside the cabin. It was really dangerous and it was probable the ship connections would be opened and it would be broken down. We had worn the life jackets and had tied ourselves to the broken chassis not to be separated by the storm. In all those critical moments, it was just God invoking that helped me to be calm and hopeful. For several times I took out the turquoise necklace and kissed it, and I hoped that the power of that stone protect us from the wind and storm as it had done before. Angela was very frightened but she tried to pretend she was calm. I had hugged her. The heavy rain and hard blowing wind had caused we could not hear one another but I ensured her that we would survive of that storm. That night it was stormy and the rain started at midnight. I was so tired that I did not know when I had got sleep.

When I opened my eyes the storm had finished and everywhere was calm as if nothing had happened for a hundred years. Angela was sleeping on the deck. I left her and checked out our situation. The storm had taken much of the food into the sea. We had only those things already tied to the chassis and the wall of the ship. All the connections and nodes had been loosed, and I was sure the next storm would damage the ship completely. A little later Angela got up and came beside me. Looking at the sea, she said "I never thought to see such a beautiful morning". Then she put her hands on her waist and said "So! Let me see what we have for breakfast" and she started to search the reminded vats. Everything was in a mess. I arranged the stuffs, took the paddles to begin paddling, but I was too hungry and tired to do so. I threw them aside and sat down in front of the ship. Angela came with a little dried fruit and smoked fish, all completely wet. She sat down beside me. I was looking at her and the food. I could not believe we had still something to eat after the storm of the last night. She bit one of the fish and said 'I think these are the most delicious food that we can eat before death". And she continued with a smile, "There is nothing to eat. This is the last food we eat before death".

After the breakfast, we checked out all the things reminded after the storm; two paddles, a fishing lance, one of the rifles with two bullets, a binoculars and a wine vat. Many of the vats, including food and drinks, had fallen into the sea or had been broken. We had nothing to eat and we had to eat just raw fish. Biting a piece of the smoked fish, Angela pointed to the wine vat Jim had given and asked "How many days we can live with this wine?".

- "I don't think that it can feed us, we only can drink too much not to know how we would die", I said while laughing.

She thought I was serious and got annoyed. I touched her face and said "Don't worry! They will rescue us, be sure". When she was calm I added "During the days when it is hot we will take a rest and watch the ships, when it is cool at nights we will paddle until morning".

-"If it does not rain for a few days, we will die of thirst, won't we?", she said.

-"Don't worry! We can swallow fish every day to survive even if we have nothing to eat or drink. And the wine Jim has made includes sugar that supplies our bodies needed energy", I said.

-"I wish I had goat milk here now. What are our friends doing now?", she sighed and said.

-"I don't know, but I am sure they think that we died, they bless our soul", I said shaking my head. She sighed again, and throwing the pieces of the broken vats which had been scattered on the deck, she said "we worked hard to make all these and now a storm has damaged all". Then throwing up and down a piece of the broken vat she asked" Yahsar! Don't you think that we should stay on the island. I never fear of death, but imagine what will happen to all those jewels we have hidden on the island if we die? Maybe for many years, nobody can find them".

Making a canopy with the reminded bamboos, I said "Seems you have not forgotten the island yet. Why don't you want to accept that we belong to another world?".

She came and sat beside me, looked at me and said "If you knew what a beautiful world I had made with you on the island, you would never say this, I wish I had got married with you and stayed there forever". When I finished the canopy, I sat down beside her and said "Angela, you are one of the girls my heart beats for, I wanted to live with you, but you know better than anybody else that I .....", she interrupted me and said "Yeah! I know you are married and want to come back to live with your family. I hope you will be happy together, but you should know I will wait for you forever". I smiled and said "You are crazy". She touched her stomach and said something in her mother tongue that I could not understand.

That day we were busy to clean up the ship until noon, then we caught some fish for lunch and dinner. It was disgusting for Angela to swallow the raw fish, but with a glass of wine after the lunch it was delightful. When it got hot, we went under the canopy to avoid sweating and thirst. We took a rest until the afternoon and watched over all around, but there was no ship. When it got dark and the stars were seen, we found the north way easily and started to paddle.

Saving angels

The next day I got up early as I was hungry, I searched around the ship, but there was no fish, so I took the fishing lance and jumped into the water to catch some fish before Angela would get up. I swam under water for a while and I could catch one fish for the breakfast. When I came up the ship I saw Angela with teary eyes standing by the fence. She had got up and as she had not seen me she was worried and had begun to cry. I took her shoulders and said "Forgive me, I just wanted to ......", she interrupted me and said "Didn't think that I will worry you?". She hugged me and started to cry again, she was right, I did wrong and if I was her I had a heart attack.

We passed the day with no especial event. Late at night we were both thirsty and hungry. The wine had made Angela to suffer from stomachache, unfortunately we had no medicine to lessen its pain, I had taken her in my arms all the night and fondling her, I could not do anything for her and I had a bad feeling. The next day the sea was a little wavy and it was so foggy that we could not see around us. We were very hungry and Angela still had the stomachache. She had laid down on the deck and was suffering from the pain. Although we were both very hungry, I could not leave her alone to catch a fish. I was really disappointed and confused. I started to cry. For a moment I looked up and called God, I said "Oh God! I can't stand anymore. How long do you want to bother us? Weren't all these problems enough?" Stop the game!", then I shot the last two bullets with irritation. Angela looked at me with a surprise, I looked down and again started to cry. Then she came beside me and while suffering from stomachache she touched my face and said" My darling! I hear a sound". While she was crying she said "surely they are angels, they are here to welcome us. We will die soon". I cleaned my tears and said "There is no sound, we will be rescued, and we will not die soon". Then I hugged her. A little later we heard the sound of a horn of a ship from a far distance. At first I thought I had made a mistake, but then I could hear the ship motor sound. The sound was louder and louder and I was sure there was a ship moving around, but it was foggy and I could not see it or guess the distance. I wanted help with a loud voice, but there was no reply. The sound was closer and closer, but nothing was seen. Again, I heard the ship horn and then a full silence. There was no sound of the motor. I thought they had not noticed our presence again and they had already passed us. I was angry and I hit the broken chassis of the ship and shouted "Oh, my God! Why do you want this?". Meanwhile, I heard a woman speaking in Russian. She asked "Is anybody there? Who are you??". They had heard us and had stopped the ship to be sure of our presence. That woman repeated her question and I replied her in Russian. Due to dense fog they could not see us, so I took out my shirt, wrapped around a piece of bamboo and fired it. A little later an orange color rescue boat with a few sailors was in front of our ship. They were angels from God. After the plane crash and arriving at the island, this was the third time that I thought I had been born again. We were rescued after one year and sixteen days.

The ship that had found us was a Japanese one with many biologists and scientists from all over the world doing research and scientific experiments about special species of fish. They could not accompany us to Indonesia due to their important missions; therefore the next day we got into an Indian cargo ship which was going to Indonesia. It was eight when we arrived at Jakarta port, the capital of Indonesia. The news of our arrival had already spread and many people, officials and reporters had come to see us, interview with us and take our photo. Among them, I could see 'Nader Hamza Ughlo', Azerbaijan charge the affairs of the embassy who welcomed us with a wreath. I was very excited, quite beside myself with joy. That I could see my family soon had made me excited. Feeling the excitement of the welcoming ceremony, I saw Angela for a while. She was worried and at that moment I had not concerned her that she was bothered of separation from me. After a short interview we went to a hotel and took part in a dinner that was for our arrival. On the way to the hotel I asked the charge the affairs of the embassy several times to contact with my wife and inform her that I was there, but he said "Don't hurry up, tomorrow morning you will talk to her, enjoy yourself tonight". That night the mayor and the governor of the city had been invited as well. Angela had sat beside the governor and was talking to him in her mother tongue. They were speaking in their mother tongue and we could not understand anything of that, but the way of their looking at me with a surprise and admiration cleared that she was talking about the works I had done on the island. When she gave the identity cards of the buried corpses to them, she whispered something to the governor that suddenly he jumped into the air and looked at me with a great surprise. He came closer and pats me on the back and said in English to all "We honor a hero here", and took me in his arms. I looked at Angela and she smiled. I guessed that she had told the story of destroying the pirates' ship. We talked until midnight and we decided to fly to the island together with the rescue team to bring our friends if the weather was good. When the guests left the dinner, I wanted to contact with my wife. The embassy charge the affairs were excusing all the time and believed that my family had already heard the news of our arrival and I should contact with them in a proper time. But when he faced with my insistence, he sat beside me and while looking down, he said, "We have already contacted. I am sorry, but I should say that your wife lost her life in an accident a few months before". Hearing this bad news I lost my control and fell down.

When I opened my eyes, I found myself on a bed in a hospital and a nurse with almond-shaped eyes, was beside me. I remembered the bad news of the last night and I got a headache again. I could not believe the end of the story would be so bad. I remembered the dream that my wife wanted me to come back soon. Poor lady! Surely it was during the death that I dreamed her asking my help. Reminding all the problems they had faced in my absence made me cry a lot.

That day I was sick and I could not accompany the rescue group to the island. I went to the airport to come back to my country. I was very sad as I could not fare well Angela. She was my good friend in all good and bad days. Before getting into the plane, the charge of the affairs of the embassy came to see me. He thanked me again for all the works I had done so far and then gave me a letter and said "this is the letter from the lady that was with you". I was not in a good mood to read it so I out it in my bag and got on the plane. When the plane took off, I remembered all the events happened during my life on the island and I cried a little. The next passenger who was from Turkey and had noticed my tears tapped on my lap and said "My friend, I know what you are thinking about. It is difficult for me to leave all these beauties too". Leaning on the chair, he said "how beautiful it was, all enjoyment and happiness". I thought the word "enjoyment", he did not know all the problems I had during this time.

It was five in the morning when I arrived in Baku airport and encountered many people come to welcome me. My brothers and sisters were there, also the families of my friends had come to get news from their husbands. Once I joined them Ramiz's wife got my cloth and asked "what about my husband? The others? Do you know anything about them?". At that moment I was not good and I could not talk to her. So without anything I just shook my head and left them. The presence of the reporters and photographers made me feel excited but I could not believe my wife's death. I was looking around with teary eyes to find her among the crowd. I was crying for her and people were thinking the tears were due to happiness. They were kissing me and appreciating me as a hero. A few hours later I went to my little sister's house. After my wife lost her life, my little sister had been taking care of my son "Oktay". He was still sleeping so I did not wake him up, I kissed him and slept beside.

Tomorrow morning, having the breakfast, my sister's husband gave me the morning newspaper and said "Man! What did you do!?". The front page of all the newspapers of Baku had written about me, and on one of them, I could read "The hero is coming back". That day all the friends and relatives were in my sister's house to see me and ask all about the events happened. I had sat down with my little son, the only thing I had from the life; touching his hair I tried to give a short reply to the questions. I didn't like to waste my time for them too much, I preferred to see my wife's grave. I was restless and my sister asked the guests to permit us and then we left the house.

When we arrived at the cemetery, I saw the reporters and journalists who had already been there and once they saw us, they surrounded me for an interview, but I ignored them and sat down beside my wife's grave and began crying. There was the date of her death on the gravestone, the same date that I had dreamed her. That night many television channels had broadcasted the scene of my crying beside my wife's grave and later on I heard that many people had cried watching the program.

A few days later I took part in one of the television programs and explained the whole story, all the events happened to us during our travel. Following that program I faced with lots of letters, telephone calls and emails. During the days I was working in the refinery and in the afternoon I was reading the emails. People all over the world were writing to me and feeling sympathy, they usually asked me to write a book about my adventurous journey; even an Italian film director suggested me to make a film about the story but due to my depression I rejected it. Even the embassy of America, Japan and Turkey had sent me citations to appreciate my activities. The consulate of Turkey in Azerbaijan issued me an honorary citizenship of their country.

During the first month I had several contacts with Demet, Hakan and Jim. But I had no news from Angela. Day by day, I got much more fame and wealth. One day I was controlling my wife's stuff when I found a bank account note with few hundred million deposits. It was strange that how she had got all that money. But a few questions from the bank revealed everything. Before my travel, I had opened a life and accident insurance account as one of my friends had suggested. When the news of the plane crash had been broadcasted, the insurance company had paid the money to my wife's account, and now I had the money instead of my poor wife.

Angela comes to wish

Three months passed and little by little I missed Angela. One day I remembered the letter she had written me. I found it among my stuff. She had written it in her mother tongue and I could not understand anything of that. I gave it to be translated, maybe I could find her address to contact. Reading the translated letter I was shocked. She had talked about an unbelievable issue and I had to find her as soon as possible. Although I had no address from her, I knew that she was studying medicine at a university in Padang. So I had a ticket for the first flight to Indonesia.

Padang was one of the important cities of Indonesia with its four schools of medicine. Surely to find Angela among all those students was a difficult job. However, when I was introducing myself to the university officials, they were happy to see me and did their best to find Angela. It was the fourth day of my residence that I went to the national university of Padang and found Angela there. She was so famous there, that even the staff of the university guard house knew her. The chancellor of the university welcomed me warmly and said "We had heard many things about Angela's husband and we were interested in seeing him sooner than this". Hearing these words I got confused and thought maybe Angela had got married and the university president had made a mistake. I got the address and left his room. I was shocked when I see a lot of the students were behind the door of the president's room and looking at me with a surprise. It was clear that everybody had heard the news in the university.

When I left the university I was in doubt to meet Angela or not, on the one hand, I could not believe whatever she had written in her letter, on the other hand I thought that she had got married. I did not want to follow what she had written in the letter and make a problem for her. I did not know what I should do. Finally, I decided to see her at least one time. I went to a dormitory where a student came and said with a smile " Hello!, you are a foreigner, aren't you? May I help you?".

-"I am Yashar, I am here to meet Angela", I said.

Suddenly she shouted "oh my God! Angela's husband! Angela's husband", and hurried into the dormitory. To be honest, I got worried at first and thought maybe Angela had got married and was living with her husband there. So before the student came back, I went to the café opposite of the dormitory. From there I saw that student together with some others was looking around to find me. I understood that I should not meet Angela so I wrote a note for her and gave it to the waiters of the café to deliver to Angela; then I went to the airport and got a ticket to Jakarta to come back to my homeland with the first flight. I was very sad because the long journey was without any result.

The flight was two hours later and I was looking at the passengers passing by the corridors, most of them had almond shaped eyes. I remembered the moment when for the first time I saw Angela in the plane. She had got all my attention and had touched my heart. Remembering all the times I had passed with her I cried. Being with her was the best part of my life. I wished I had never seen her. I was busy thinking when he loudspeaker announced the flight to Jakarta. I stood up with a broken heart and took my luggage to go to the exit gate when I heard a voice calling me, "Yashar". At first I thought I had made a mistake, but when I turned back, I saw Angela with lots of the university students with a smile and astonished eyes behind me. For a moment I was shocked and thought I had made a mistake, but Angela called me "Yashar! My darling", then she hugged me. When I realized everything was true, I threw the luggage aside and hugged her. Although I am a shy person, regardless of all the crowds and their clapping, I had hugged her and was kissing her repeatedly. While she was crying, she said "I knew you would come back, I will never let you leave me, Yashar!".

That night I invited Angela and all her friends in the dormitory for dinner in the restaurant of the hotel I was staying. The dinner party including music and fireworks was so great that other tourists were recording films, they were thinking that it was the marriage ceremony of one of the princess of the Arabic countries. I was so happy to see Angela again that I wanted to drink wine and enjoy myself until morning.

That night Angela stayed with me in the hotel and we talked until morning. That night I understood that she had written me the truth and she was pregnant. It was unbelievable, but when she told the story of that mysterious drink on the second week of leaving the island I knew that she had made me unconscious and had run her dirty plan. Arriving at her homeland, she had told everybody the whole of the story and to avoid any problem in the future she had said we had already got married. When I asked why she had done all these she cried and said "You were so good that I would not want to lose you. When I saw I could never keep you on the island I thought I should have a child from you. You were decided to stay with your family and I could not stand to lose you, so I did my best in a proper time and now I have a child from you. When I hug your child, I will feel your presence beside me".

Two days later I got married to Angela and she got her dream. The news of our marriage was published in many newspapers in Indonesia and many television channels interviewed with us. The journey that I thought would take one week ended after seventy days and during this time another interesting event happened that I could not imagine even in my dreams. When I had come back to my homeland, Angela had delivered all the treasure we had already found on the island, to the government officials in her motherland and had asked the island itself as a gift. When she got the property documents of the island she was very excited and was talking all the time about the plans she had for the future life. She wanted me to go to the island and live there forever, but I did not agree with this. After five months she gave birth our pretty daughter and to remember all the nights we had spent together on the wharf we called her Yakamooz or the reflection of the moon on water. Her birth made our life happier than before. We were living most of the time in Azerbaijan and travelling to Indonesia we were going to our own island for the memory of all joyful time we had there.

Then after, one of my friends had an interesting suggestion that we could run an international competition and anybody who could live alone on the island for six months with no facilities, he would win a big money. This work needed lots of money to purchase cameras and telecommunication systems to record and broadcast the program that we did not have. On the other hand, I did not like to share the work with an investor, so Angela solved the problem with her good intelligence.

When we had found the treasure on the island we had divided it into two parts and had hidden them into different sections. When we were rescued, I had recommended her to deliver the whole of the treasure to Indonesia government, but she had given just half of the treasure and had kept the rest for herself. Selling the treasure we could run the competition the next year. Our competition called "Six months life like Robinson Cruise" had been advertised throughout the world and so far thirty individuals have registered however all have failed. This television program with its many audiences throughout the world is broadcasted alive. The money earned through the program selling is used to build schools, hospitals and other charitable works in Indonesia and some other African countries.

Now that I am writing this story I have an enjoyable life with my good wife, Angela, and my children, Oktay and Yakamooz, and I owe all these to the island. The island, that one day I thought would lead me to death in the far alien land was a bed for my progress and success. Now I know that in every story there is wisdom of God and every happening even the worst one could result in the best outcome.

The end.